**Françoise Lemarchand**
Professeur agrégé
Lycée-collège Victor Duruy, Paris

**Kathleen Julié**
Maître de conférences
Université de Paris-Sorbonne

# Spring

## Anglais 5e

CYCLE CENTRAL

**Jean-Rémi Lapaire**
Professeur de linguistique
Université de Toulouse-Le Mirail

**Jean-Robert Perrin**
Professeur agrégé
Collège André Maurois, Limoges
Formateur IUFM du Limousin

**Marie-Pierre Butts-Pasquini**
Professeur agrégé
Collège Fontcarrade, Montpellier
PhD Yale University

**Paul Butts**
Professeur certifié
MA Chicago University

HACHETTE
Éducation

# Préface aux élèves

Tu entres en 5e. Tu es plein(e) d'énergie. Cela tombe bien. Te rappelles-tu de tous les sens du mot *SPRING* ?

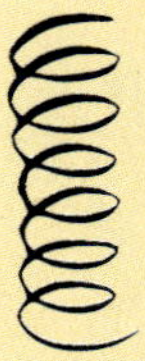   

Cette année tu vas retrouver les amis du club de théâtre de Mark à Londres. Il y a un nouveau, Kevin, et certains sont repartis, dont Ben, que tu vas suivre en Californie.

Jim Ricotti court toujours, enfin, jusqu'à l'*Epilogue*.

Ton livre comprend cinq *Acts* hormis le *Prologue* au début (transition avec la 6e) et l'*Epilogue*, à la fin, (transition facultative avec la 4e).

Comme l'année dernière, le génie de la langue, *Magic Lingo*, te donne rendez-vous dans les *Scenes* 1 et 3 de chaque *Act*, et dans ton *Workbook*. Avec lui, la grammaire devient un jeu !

Et grâce aux cinq *Workshop*, tu vas pouvoir fabriquer des objets, créer des dossiers et jouer, en anglais bien sûr !

Enfin, cette année, tu dois pouvoir lire pour le plaisir. À la fin de ton manuel tu trouveras donc deux histoires complètes à découvrir.

N'oublie pas non plus les chansons patrimoines et les poèmes rigolos.

Alors, bonne année avec *SPRING* 5e !

Les auteurs

Ce livre est dédié à Perrine.

**Conception graphique** : Sarbacane, Marion Fernagut
**Mise en page** : Marion Fernagut
**Illustrations** : Bruno Le Sourd, Philippe Chauvet
**Couverture** : Sarbacane ; **illustration** : Eric Héliot
**Cartographie** : Hachette Éducation

**Références des textes et illustrations** : voir en page 184.

ISBN : 2-01-125274-1

# The Sounds of English

**Les symboles phonétiques représentent les sons de l'anglais. Voici ceux que tu dois connaître.**

## VOYELLES

[ə]
Les voyelles 'décolorées' : on les entend à peine.

## CONSONNES

**Les sons consonnes sont représentés par les lettres de l'alphabet [b], [t], etc., sauf pour :**

| [θ] | [ð] | [ʃ] | [tʃ] | [ʒ] | [dʒ] | [ŋ] | [j] |
|---|---|---|---|---|---|---|---|
| **th**ree | **th**e | **sh**oe | **ch**air | bei**g**e | **j**am | ri**ng** | **y**ellow |

# Table des matières

- fonctions
- grammaire
- lexique

*PLACEMENT TEST sur cassette seulement - PLACEMENT TEST sur cassette seulement - PLACEMENT TEST*

# Table des matières

Chaque *Act* est suivi soit d'une évaluation-bilan, soit d'un test (fichier d'utilisation).



→

# Table des matières

- fonctions
- grammaire
- lexique

# Table des matières

Chaque *Act* est suivi soit d'une évaluation-bilan, soit d'un test (fichier d'utilisation).

# Un Act de Spring 5^e^

**INTÉGRATION DES OBJECTIFS ET CONSTRUCTION EN SPIRALE**

## PAGE D'OUVERTURE

**Contrat d'apprentissage**
Repris dans le *Workbook* (page d'ouverture de l'*Act* et page de révision).

## Setting the scene

**Réactivation d'un point de grammaire du programme de 6^e^.**
**Élargissement lexical par l'œil, l'oreille, la plume.**

- Associations de mots et de dessins par une écoute interactive *(Wb).*
- Mini-dialogue avec repérage du lexique nouveau *(Wb).*
- Transfert dans la classe.
- *Think and store*: travail personnel (réemploi) + *Forget-me-not* interactif *(Wb).*

Grammar Basics
- Résumé grammatical + exercices d'application (+ *Exercise bank).*

## scene 1

Show you know
- Mobilisation des acquis pour vérification.

Discover more
- Préparation à l'écoute et anticipation à partir d'un commentaire d'image.
- Écoute du dialogue , prise de notes, formulation et commentaire (*Wb*).

Your turn now
- Premiers pas vers l'autonomie en production orale.

Magic Lingo
- Réflexion grammaticale sur cassette et dans le *Workbook*.
- Travail phonétique sur le message de *Magic Lingo (Wb).*

Think and store
- Travail personnel *(Wb)* ; aide à la mémorisation et *Forget-me-not* interactif.

Grammar Basics
- Résumé grammatical + exercices d'application (+ *Exercise bank).*

## scene 2

**Élargissement grammatical et lexical, intégration de l'objectif culturel.**

Show you know
- Mobilisation des acquis pour vérification.

Spring into action
- Découverte d'un document souvent authentique en expression orale autonome.
- Mini-écoute interactive pour introduire le fait de langue nouveau *(Wb).*
- Appropriation en *class work, group work, pair work*.
- Reprise du fait de langue dans une écoute sans support visuel *(Wb), avec* travail d'anticipation à partir de bribes enregistrées.
- Transfert en production orale.
- Mise en plume du fait de langue dans une mini-rédaction personnalisée.

Think and store
- Travail personnel *(Wb),* réemploi + *Forget-me-not* interactif.

Grammar Basics
- Résumé grammatical + exercices d'application (+ *Exercise bank).*

## scene 3 scene 4

**Construction identique aux scènes 1 & 2.**

## Put pen to paper

**Learn to write better** - À partir de modèles, apprendre à rédiger et à corriger ses erreurs.
**Write it yourself** - Rédaction autonome avec aide dans le *Workbook*.

## scene 5

**Lecture et civilisation**

**What do you know?** - Introduction du thème et *brainstorming* à partir de ce que les élèves savent.
- Stratégies d'observation *(Wb)*.

**Prepare to read** - Aide lexicale et anticipation *(Wb)*.

**Spring into English** - Stratégies de lecture :
page de gauche, niveau 1 *(Wb)*.
page de droite, niveau 2 *(Wb)* + *Listen*, élargissement du thème de civilisation *(Wb)*.

## Encore

**Révision du chapitre**

**React** - Réactivation à partir d'un support iconographique : prise de parole autonome.
**Read** - Réactivation par la lecture, repérage des mots clefs à l'écrit *(Wb)*.
**Listen** - Réactivation par une écoute, repérage des mots clefs à l'oral *(Wb)*.
**Phonetics** - Phonèmes, rythme et accentuation, intonation.
**Dictation** - Préparation sur la cassette et dans le *Workbook*.

## Oral recap. Word builder

Réactivation orale du lexique vu dans l'*Act*, travail sur la formation des mots.

## workshop

**Do-it-yourself** - *Learning by doing.*
**On the net** - Proposition de recherche sur un thème en rapport avec l'*Act*.
**Project** - Expression écrite créative.
**Game** - Fabrication d'un jeu pour jouer en classe.
***Workbook*** - Lecture sur l'un des thèmes de civilisation de l'*Act*

**TABLEAU RÉCAPITULATIF DES COMPÉTENCES DE COMMUNICATION MISES EN ŒUVRE DANS UN *ACT****

| | compréhension orale | production orale expression orale | compréhension écrite | Production écrite expression écrite |
|---|---|---|---|---|
| Setting the scene | ++ | ++ | | + |
| Scenes 1 et 3 | +++ | +++ | + | + |
| Scenes 2 et 4 | +++ | +++ | + | ++ |
| Put pen to paper | | | + | +++ |
| Scene 5 | ++ | + | +++ | + |
| Encore | ++ | ++ | ++ | + |
| Oral recap. | | + | | |
| Workshop | | ++ | +++ | +++ |

* Les "+" indiquent l'importance accordée à chaque compétence.

# PROLOGUE

## DANS CES DIX ACTIVITÉS

### TU VAS T'EXERCER

- à te présenter.
- à te renseigner sur l'identité et les origines d'un camarade.
- à épeler.
- à dire la date et l'heure.
- à échanger des numéros de téléphone.

### TU VAS REVOIR

- le verbe *"be"*.
- *"this / that"*.
- *"who? what? where ... from? how old?"*
- les chiffres et les nombres jusqu'à 100.
- l'alphabet.

# Me, now, here ...

# Let's meet again!

- FAIS CONNAISSANCE AVEC TES CAMARADES.
- PARLE DE NATIONALITÉS ET D'ORIGINES.

1

2

3

4

## 5

**a. Say where they are from. Then guess the city where they live.**

Jason

Clara

Pamela

Sean

**b. Listen. What cities are they really from? What are their origins?**

## 6

**a. Talk about origins in the class. Then colour the countries.**

**b. Write a poem with names or origins. Find a rhythm or a rhyme.**

*We are in 5F.*
*F for Frank and F for Fanny.*
*From Amaury to Stephanie,*
*From Thierry to Virginie,*
*It is the class for me!*

*Where are the 5F from?*
*From Asia and from America.*
*From Algeria and from India.*
*From Togo and from Sri Lanka.*
*That's where the 5F are from!*

## forget-me-not

**Vérifie que tu sais...** - dire ton nom, ta nationalité, ton origine.
- interroger un camarade à ce sujet.

Sean Connery is from Scotland. He is Scottish, isn't he?

**Rappelle-toi :** cinq nationalités (représentées dans ta classe).

### "BE"

**Affirmation**
**+**

I **am** — I'm
You **are** — You're
He / She / It **is** — He's

**Question**
**?**

**Am** I?
**Are** you?
**Is** he / she / it?

**Négation**
**–**

I **am not**. — I'm not.
You **are not**. — You aren't.
He / She / It **is not**. — He isn't.

# Letters and numbers

▶ RÉVISE L'ALPHABET ET LES NOMBRES.
▶ DIS L'HEURE ET LA DATE.

**7** a. Listen, say the alphabet and then play games with letters.

b. Study the Semaphore signalling code. Then mime a letter or a word. The class says it.

c. Are any letters of the alphabet missing in this sentence? Check, starting with "A".

The quick brown fox jumps over the lazy dog.

**8** **a. Listen: play with numbers and then draw the time.**
**b. What time is it?**

**9** **a. Listen: when are their birthdays?**
**b. Say when your birthday is and make a birthday chart.**

## forget-me-not

**Vérifie que tu sais...** - compter et dire l'alphabet.
- demander et dire l'heure.
- dire et écrire les dates.

It is half past seven on Monday September 12th, isn't it?

**DIRE L'HEURE**

*Sauf pour l'heure juste, commence toujours par la grande aiguille.*

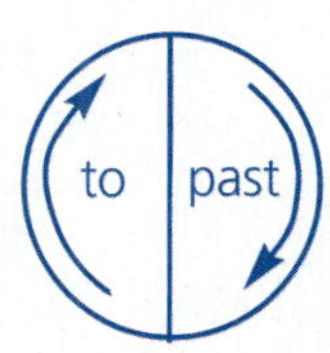


1.15: (a) quarter past one
1.30: half past one
1.45: (a) quarter to two

**Rappelle-toi :** les nombres ordinaux.
1st first 2nd second 3rd third 4th fourth 5th fifth 6th sixth, etc.

# Who are they?

▶ PRÉSENTE LES PERSONNAGES.
▶ PARLE D'ÂGES ET DE NUMÉROS DE TÉLÉPHONE.

**10** a. Say what you remember about them. Ask questions if you don't know.
b. Listen. Identify who is speaking and then find out more about them.

**c. Sing the Spring song.**

## forget-me-not

**Vérifie que tu sais...** - présenter un(e) camarade.
- poser des questions sur l'âge.
- demander et dire un numéro de téléphone.

Kevin is twelve and a half, isn't he?

**SE RENSEIGNER**

*sur l'identité*
**Who** is that girl?

*sur les origines*
**Where** is she **from**?

*sur l'âge*
**How old** is she?

*sur une chose*
**What** is her telephone number?

**Rappelle-toi :** ces liens de famille.
mother - father - stepmother - stepfather - brother - sister - half-brother - half-sister

# Grammar

## BE

**Présenter, décrire : dire ce qui fait partie de la personne et la définit.**
– dire qui on est : I am Kevin ou My name is Kevin.
– dire ce qu'on est : Ian is British (nationalité) ; He is a teacher (profession) ; You are 12 (âge), etc.
– dire comment on est : I am 1.80 m (taille) ; She's clever (qualité).

**Localiser : situer la personne dans l'espace.**
– dire où on est : Where are you? I'm here.
– dire d'où on est : Where is Rob from? He's from London.

| + | ? | − |
|---|---|---|
| I am. | Am I? | I am not. |
| You are. | Are you? | You are not. |
| He / She / It is. | Is he? / she? / it? | He / She / It is not. |
| We / You / They are. | Are we? / you? / they? | We / You / They are not. |

**a.** Si je te demande *"Are you French?"* que réponds-tu ?

## LES TAGS

Après avoir affirmé quelque chose, tu peux utiliser un *"tag"* :

You are English, aren't you? (+ −) François is French, isn't he? (+ −)

You are not English, are you? (− +) Mark is not French, is he? (− +)

Le *tag* (= mini-question en fin d'énoncé) a plusieurs fonctions :
- encourager le dialogue : "micro qu'on tend vers l'autre", manière de dire : "tu es là", "tu as le droit d'intervenir".
- signaler un manque de certitude : manière de dire "je ne suis pas sûr de moi".

Le *tag* est un "acte de communication" important.

**b.** Combien de fois apparaît *"not"* dans une phrase avec un *"tag"* ?

## YOU OU YOUR ?

- Avec *you*, tu t'adresses aux autres.

You are my friend(s). You are my teacher(s).

Ici, *you* (pronom personnel) est sujet du verbe *be*.

- Avec *your*, tu relies une personne, une chose à *you*.

*Your* accompagne un nom. C'est un déterminant.

Your teacher is French. Your school is beautiful.

## ENTRAÎNE-TOI

**1 Retrouve les phrases.**
1. ? / your / is / What / name
2. aren't / you /, / You / are / French / ?
3. that / This / is / is / Mary / and / Ben
4. not / from / I / Scotland / am
5. from / Where / you / ? / are

**2 *Who* ou *what* ? Complète et réponds.**
1. ... is the name of your school?
2. ... is your English teacher?
3. ... are your best friends' names?
4. ... nationality is your mother?
5. ... is your favourite actor?

**3 *Your* ou *you* ? Complète et réponds.**
1. Where is ... father from?
2. What city are ... from?
3. Where are ... school friends from?
4. ... are French, aren't ...?
5. Where do ... live? What is ... address?

**4 Retrouve la question.**
1. ...? My name is Pierre.
2. ...? I am French.
3. ...? I am from Lyon.
4. ...? It's my friend, Pierre.
5. ...? Yes, he is.

**5 *He, she* ou *it* ?**
1. Who is this boy? ... is Ben.
2. ... is American, isn't ...?
3. Who is this girl? ... is Sophie.
4. ... is from Dublin, isn't ...?
5. What is this? ... is a name tag.

**6 Où se trouvent ces villes ?**

*Ex. : Paris is in France, isn't it?*
1. Dallas
2. Edinburgh
3. Manchester
4. Cardiff
5. Dublin
6. Quebec and Montreal

**a.** *Yes, I am.* (+) ou *No, I'm not.* (-) Tu reprends *be*, qui est dans la question. Tu évites ainsi de dire seulement Yes ou No (très secs). **b.** *Not* apparaît une seule fois.

# Grammar

MORE!
▶ EXERCISE BANK, P. 161
▶ GRAMMAR STORE, P. 142

## THIS / THAT

*This* et *that* permettent d'attirer l'attention et sont très utiles dans les présentations.

This is Julie and that is James.

⚠ Question avec *this / that*, réponse avec *it* !

Who is this (man)? It's my friend Paul.

## LES "WH" QUESTIONS

- *Who, what, where, how* sont des mots interrogatifs. Ils "lancent" la question et se placent donc au début.
- *Wh-* transmet toujours le même message : "J'ai besoin d'une information précise sur un point particulier."

| Questions | Je cherche à savoir ... |
|---|---|
| Who is this girl? What is her name? | l'identité, le nom. |
| Where are you from? | le lieu d'origine. |

Quelle question me poses-tu pour savoir mon âge ?

## L'HEURE

*PAST* : la grande aiguille s'éloigne de l'heure ancienne.
*TO* : la grande aiguille s'approche de l'heure nouvelle.
Logique ! *PAST* : de *pass* "dépasser".
*TO* : "aller vers"

| | |
|---|---|
| L'heure juste | It is 9 o'clock. |
| Les minutes qui dépassent (jusqu'à 30) | It is ten past nine. |
| Le quart (on dépasse d'un quart) | It is a quarter past nine. |
| La demi (on dépasse d'un demi) | It is half past nine. |
| Les minutes qui manquent | It is twenty to ten. |
| Moins le quart (il manque un quart) | It is a quarter to ten. |

## LA DATE

- **Tu dis :**

"the $12^{th}$ of september" ou "September the $12^{th}$"

- **Tu écris :** September 12th / 12th September / September 12.

| | | | | | |
|---|---|---|---|---|---|
| $1^{st}$ | the first | $6^{th}$ | the sixth | $11^{th}$ | the eleventh |
| $2^{nd}$ | the second | $7^{th}$ | the seventh | $12^{th}$ | the twelfth |
| $3^{rd}$ | the third | $8^{th}$ | the eighth | $13^{th}$ | the thirteenth |
| $4^{th}$ | the fourth | $9^{th}$ | the ninth | $14^{th}$ | the fourteenth |
| $5^{th}$ | the fifth | $10^{th}$ | the tenth | $15^{th}$ | the fifteenth |
| $20^{th}$ | the twentieth | $21^{st}$ | the twenty-first, etc. | | |
| $30^{th}$ | the thirtieth | $31^{st}$ | the thirty-first, etc. | | |

## ENTRAÎNE-TOI

**7 Écris ces nombres cardinaux en lettres.**

1. → 33
2. → 44
3. → 55
4. → 78
5. → 92
6. → 84

**8 Écris ces nombres ordinaux en lettres.**

1. → $22^{nd}$
2. → $33^{rd}$
3. → $44^{th}$
4. → $89^{th}$
5. → $12^{th}$
6. → $31^{st}$

**9 Écris les heures.**

1. 2. 3. 4. 5.

**10 Retrouve la question.**

1. ...? It's Monday.
2. ...? It's on December $3^{rd}$.
3. ...? It's half past one.
4. ...? 03 489 85647.
5. ...? He's from Toulouse.

**11 Demande leur âge et invente une réponse logique.**

**12 Qui sont-ils ? Rattache-les à une personne. (Voir le génitif, p. 30)**

*Ex.* : Shawna (Sophie)
→ *Shawna is Sophie's sister.*

1. Mr Martin (Aliette)
2. Mrs Macguire (Sophie)
3. Juliet (Ian)
4. Ian (James)
5. Steve (Sophie)

Tu dis : "How old are you?" "How old" interroge donc sur l'âge.

# ACT 1

## DANS CE CHAPITRE

### TU VAS T'EXERCER

- à nommer des objets et les décrire.
- à dire à qui appartient tel ou tel objet.
- à parler de toi, de ta famille et de ton école.
- à décrire ce qui se passe au moment où tu parles.
- à lire pour découvrir d'autres écoles à travers le monde.

### TU VAS REVOIR

- *"be", "have got".*
- le présent simple.
- *"be + -ing".*

### TU VAS UTILISER

- le vocabulaire de l'école.
- quelques adjectifs pour parler de tes qualités et défauts.
- quelques verbes pour donner un itinéraire.

# School days

# Setting the scene

▶ NOMME DES OBJETS DE LA CLASSE.
▶ DÉCRIS-LES.
▶ DIS À QUI ILS APPARTIENNENT.

## School things

- Talk about the objects. Compare with yours. Ask questions.

- Play and learn new words.
- Show you understand: the "feelie bag".
- Your turn now!

a. Play the "feelie-bag game".

b. Make riddles.

**HELP!**

square

round

rectangular

pointed

long ≠ short

hard ≠ soft

## forget-me-not

**Vérifie que tu sais...** - parler d'objets que tu utilises en classe.
- dire à qui appartient tel ou tel objet.

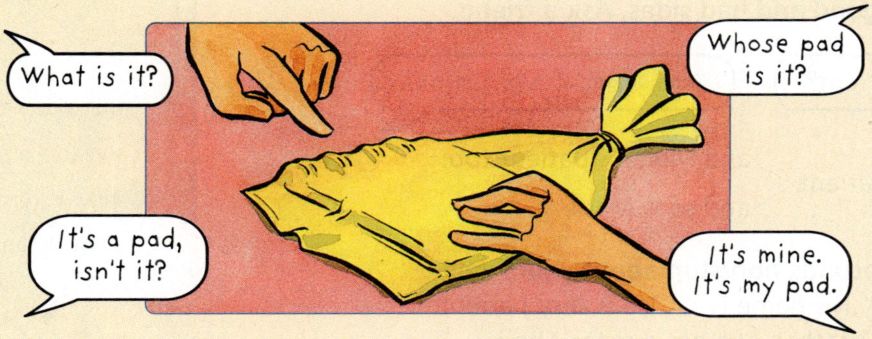


This pad is Marie's, isn't it? Yes, it is.

**WHOSE IS IT?**

Is it [ your pen? / yours?

Yes, it is [ my pen. / mine.

**Rappelle-toi :** au moins cinq mots nouveaux utiles pour la classe.

# scene 1

▶ PARLE DE TOI, DE TA FAMILLE, DE QUALITÉS ET DE DÉFAUTS.

## 1 SHOW YOU KNOW

- **Classroom objects: test your friends' memories.**
- **Make a riddle. The class guesses.**

## 2 DISCOVER MORE

- **Look and say what you can. Don't forget to ask questions.**

- **Listen for information about the teacher.**

## 3 YOUR TURN NOW!

- **Talk about your good and bad sides. Ask a friend.**

Are you patient?

Yes, I am. / No, I'm not.

- **Conclude.** I am patient — and Marie is patient too. / and so is Marie.

- **Talk for fifteen seconds non-stop about your family.**
  A: My father is ... . His name is ... . He is very patient.
  B: I haven't got a brother. I've got a sister. She is ... .

- **Magic Lingo: I'm back!**

**HELP!**

good-**temp**ered

quiet ≠ talkative

**so**ciable ≠ shy

tidy ≠ messy

handy ≠ clumsy

I've got a nose but I'm not nosy! I've got two hands but I'm not handy!

## THINK AND STORE

**1** **Read and imagine the scene. Make sure you understand everything.**

**Mr Uccles** : Good morning. Sit down. Let me introduce myself. I'm your English teacher. My name is Ian Christopher Uccles. Call me Mr. ICU. *(laughter)* Well, have you got any questions?
**Kevin** : Are you strict, Sir?
**Mr ICU** : Only when my pupils are rude or lazy. But I am patient and friendly when they are polite and hard-working.

**Sophie** : Are you married?
**Mr ICU** : Yes, I am. And I've got two children ... and a half! My wife is expecting a baby in April. A girl, I hope!
**James** : How old are your children?
**Mr ICU** : My son is 4. His name is Mike. And my daughter is 2. Her name is Laura.

**Kevin** : How old are you?
**Mr ICU** : You are nosy, aren't you? I'm 95 years old. *(laughter)* Now, Mr Nosy, introduce yourself, please!

**2** **Count all the qualifying adjectives. How many have you got?**

**3** **Open your workbook and learn your lesson step by step.**

▶ EXERCISES AND GRAMMAR: PAGE 30.

### HELP!

uː
rude: **in**solent

a hal̸f: 1/2

ʌ aɪ
**hus**band & wife

ʌ ɔː
son **daug**h̸ter

## forget-me-not

**Vérifie que tu sais...** - parler de toi, de ta famille, de qualités et de défauts.

Mr Uccles is married. He **has** got two children.
**His** son **is** four years old. **His** daughter **is** two.

**Rappelle-toi :** cinq adjectifs pour parler de qualités et de défauts.

### "HAVE"

**+**

I / You — **have** got. (I've got.)
He / She / It — **has** got. (He's got.)
We / You / They — **have** got.

**?**

**Have** you got ...?
**Has** he got ...? Etc.

**–**

I **have not** got. (I haven't got.)
He **has not** got. Etc.

# scene 2

▶ PARLE DE TON EMPLOI DU TEMPS.
▶ DIS CE QUE TU AIMES OU NON À L'ÉCOLE.

## 1 SHOW YOU KNOW

- Say what you remember about Mr ICU.
- Ask a friend about his / her personality and compare with yours.

## 2 SPRING INTO ACTION

- Look and say what you can. Ask questions.
- Listen and discover how to talk about James's timetable.

- Talk about your own timetable. Write it out.
- What is your favourite subject? Your favourite day? Why?

- **Conclude.** I like ... and X likes it too. We **both** like ... because ...
  I don't like ... and X doesn**'t** like it **either**.

- Look at the photo. What lesson is it? Listen to their problems.

- Say what your own problems are today.
- Write about the subjects you like / don't like.

## SAY IT!

regis**tra**tion

ge**o**graphy

aɪɒ
bi**o**logy

aɪ
**sci**ence

ɪ
**Tues**day

ɪ
**Wed**nesday

▶ PLAY AND LEARN IN YOUR WORKBOOK.
▶ EXERCISES AND GRAMMAR: PAGE 30.

## forget-me-not

**Vérifie que tu sais...** - parler de ton emploi du temps.
- dire ce que tu aimes ou non à l'école.

On Tuesday**s** they have geography.
James **doesn't** like it and Rob **doesn't** like it **either**.

### "LIKE"

*Parler de goûts.*

**+**
I like.
He like**s**.

**?**
**Do** you like?
**Does** he like?

**–**
I **don't** like.
He **doesn't** like.

**Rappelle-toi :** ces matières scolaires.
English - French - German - Latin - maths - science - technology
history - geography - art - music - physical education (PE)

⚠ I've forgotten it. *Oublié !* — I've lost it. *Perdu !* — I haven't done it. *Pas fait !* ≠ I've done it. *Fait !*

# scene 3

▶ DÉCRIS CE QUI SE PASSE AU MOMENT OÙ TU PARLES.
▶ RENSEIGNE-TOI.

## 1 SHOW YOU KNOW

- **Ask a friend about his / her favourite school subjects.**
- **What is your timetable today? What have you forgotten, lost, done, not done?**

## 2 DISCOVER MORE

- **Look and answer your teacher.**
  T: Who is eating? A: Kevin is. He is eating an apple, isn't he?
- **Close your book and test your friends.**
  A: What is ... doing? B: He is ... ing, isn't he? / I don't remember.

- **Listen. What are the teachers doing?** WB

## 3 YOUR TURN NOW!

- **Play "Freeze".**

- **Look at James's timetable on page 18 and listen. Find the lesson, the day, the time.**
- **Magic Lingo: Zooming in with "be + -ing"!**

"You're not listening to me, are you?" "Yes, we are!" "No, you're not!"

## THINK AND STORE

**1** **Read and imagine the scene. Make sure you understand everything.**

*It's break. The pupils are not supposed to be in the classroom. James is downstairs. Rob is talking to him on his mobile.*

**Rob** : What are the teachers doing, James?
**James** : They're having tea and biscuits in the staff room.
**Rob** : Can you see Mr ICU? What's he doing?
**James** : He is writing a letter. The music teacher is playing the piano. The French teacher is reading *Le Monde* and the science teacher is on the phone.

Look out! The Head is coming! He is turning left. He is crossing the playground! He's going upstairs!
**Rob** : Quick everyone! The Head is coming! Shhhh!

**Head** : *(Door opens.)* What are you doing here, children? Why aren't you outside?
**Sophie** : We're revising for the French test! Can we stay in, Sir?
**Head** : *May* we stay in! Well, if you are really working, you may. But be very quiet. *(Door closes. Steps. Noise starts again.)*

**HELP!**

the staff room: the teachers' room

turn left

**up**stairs

**down**stairs

to stay in
≠
to go out

PERMISSION
Can we? (polite)
May we? (more polite)

**2** **Count all the action verbs. How many have you got?**

**3** **Open your workbook and learn your lesson step by step.**

▶ EXERCISES AND GRAMMAR: PAGE 31.

## forget-me-not

**Vérifie que tu sais...** - décrire ce qui se passe au moment où tu parles.
- interroger tes camarades à ce sujet.

Rob is revising and so is James.
They aren't telephoning, are they?

**LE PRÉSENT EN "BE + -ING"**

*C'est maintenant que ça se passe !*

What **are** you do**ing** ?

**Are** you work**ing** ?
Yes I am.
No, I am not. — I'm not.

**Is** she work**ing** ?
Yes, she is.
No, she is not. — She isn't.

**Rappelle-toi :** ces actions.
**In class:** I work, I listen to the teacher, I speak, I read, I write.
**At home:** I revise, I do my homework.

# scene 4

- PARLE DE TON ÉCOLE : DES BÂTIMENTS, DES SALLES ET DU PERSONNEL.
- INDIQUE UN ITINÉRAIRE.

## 1 SHOW YOU KNOW

- Listen. What are they doing? Where are they?

## 2 SPRING INTO ACTION

- Look and say what you can. Ask questions.
- Listen and follow the directions.

**HELP!**

**WHERE?**

upstairs
downstairs
inside
outside
near
opposite
between

**DIRECTIONS**

turn left
turn right
go straight on
go past
cross

- **Give your friends directions to a mystery destination. Start from your classroom.**
  A: Turn right. Cross the ... . Go upstairs and go past the ... . Where are you?

- **Listen. Who is speaking? Check with the class.**

1 Mr Hopkins, the gardener

2 Mrs Collins, the cook

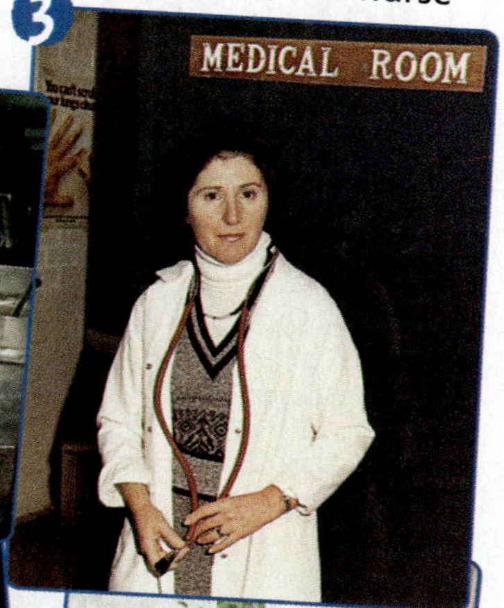


3 Miss Wade, the nurse

4 Mr Kelly, the caretaker

5 Mrs Lunt, the school cleaner

6 Mr Burton, the Head

- **Think of a person or a place in your school. Give two clues. The class guesses.**

A: We eat there. It is near / opposite ... B: It's the dining hall, isn't it?

▶ PLAY AND LEARN IN YOUR WORKBOOK.
▶ EXERCISES AND GRAMMAR: PAGE 31.

## forget-me-not

**Vérifie que tu sais...** - parler de ton école : des bâtiments, des salles, du personnel.

Sylvia Lunt is the school cleaner. She cleans the school, doesn't she?

**Rappelle-toi :** - comment indiquer le chemin pour aller de l'entrée du collège à ta salle préférée.

### LE PRÉSENT SIMPLE

*Une info simple !*

She is a cleaner.
She clean**s** the school.
She do**es** not teach.

Do**es** she cook?
No, she do**es**n't.

Who cook**s**?
The cook cook**s**.

# Put pen to paper

## 1 Learn to write better!

What is wrong? Correct in your workbook. WB

**Punctuation and capital letters**

at school i am not very happy i always imagine that the other children don't like me i am sure they think i am stupid because i am not talkative my favourite lesson is english what is yours

**Style**

Mrs Philips is the music teacher.
Mrs Philips thinks her job is very nice, because she thinks music is very nice.
Mrs Philips also thinks the pupils are very nice.

## 2 Write it yourself!

**a.** Choose one of these topics.

**ESSAY**

1. School and you.
2. Introduce somebody who works in your school.

Need help? Workbook!

**b.** Note down the ideas and the information.

**School and me!**

Happy? When? Sad? When?

places food subjects time friends teachers

I love
I adore
I like

I hate
I don't like

- Name: ..........
- Married? ..........
- Children? ..........
- Place of residence: ..........
- Job: ..........
- What he / she does: ..........
- Opinion about job: ..........
- Opinion about pupils: ..........

**c.** Write a rough copy. *(Rédige au brouillon.)*

**d.** Check the punctuation and improve your style.

**e.** Copy out your text. Be creative!

# scene 5

PARS À LA DÉCOUVERTE D'ÉCOLES DANS LE MONDE.
▶ Dis ce que tu sais.
▶ Prépare-toi.
▶ Lis.

# Lucky to be at school!

## 1 WHAT DO YOU KNOW? WB

- Who is lucky? Who isn't? Why?

1 A village school in Kenya

2 A carpet factory in Pakistan

3 Eaton: an independent school

4 A school in the USA

## 2 PREPARE TO READ WB

- Match the words and the definitions.

comprehensive schools — day schools — boarding schools — independent schools

a. They are private and independent. Parents pay.
b. They are schools where you board (live).
c. They are schools where you go every day.
d. They are for all children. Parents don't pay.

# scene 5

## 3 SPRING INTO ENGLISH

- **Reading strategies: concentrate on the photos, titles, names and words you know.**

1

### Selim

I live in Manchester and I go to Park Hill Comprehensive School.
My parents are from Pakistan and my father is a doctor.
I think I'm lucky to go to school and I love it. First of all, that is where all my friends are and secondly, we play a lot of football.
I'm football crazy and I support Manchester United, the best British team!
I am quite good at science and I love biology. When I grow up I want to be a dentist.

### Shirley

I go to an independent school in the south of England. I am a boarder because I don't want to live at home with my step-mother.
At school we do a lot of sport and we never get bored.
Every year we go to France with our French teacher and the German teacher takes us to Germany or Austria. The history teacher organises a lot of trips too. When I grow up, I certainly do not want to be a politician like my father!

2

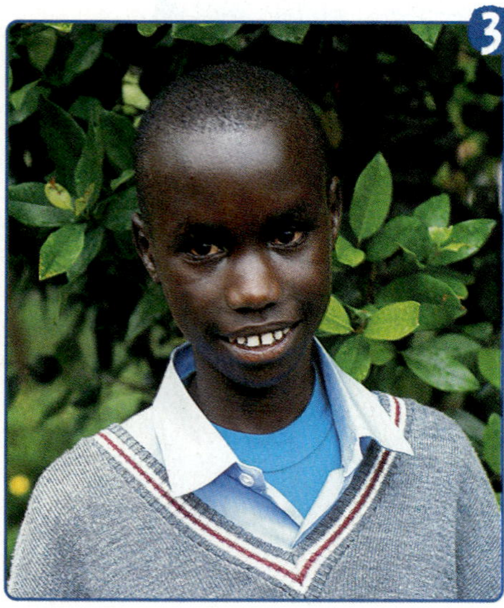

3

### Jomo

I go to a boys' school in Nairobi, the capital of Kenya, but I come from a village where my father is a farmer.
I like school because we have electricity and I have my own bed here.
All the pupils are from different villages and speak different dialects, so the lessons are in English, which is the language we have to speak at school.
When I am older, I want to live in a city and have a good job. I'd like to be a policeman.

# IQBAL MASIH
## the boy who wanted to go to school

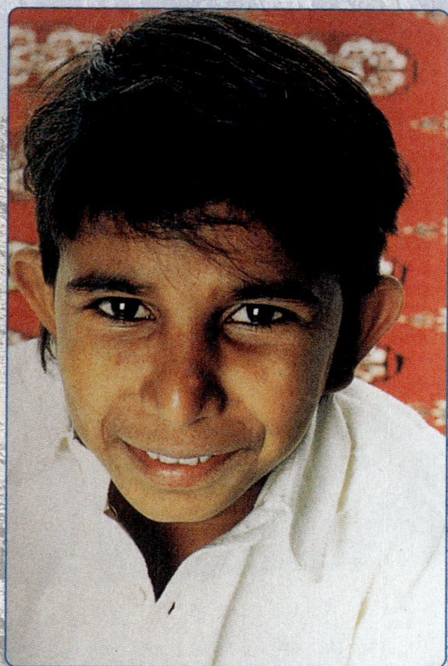

When Iqbal Masih was four years old, his father sold him for $12 to work as a slave.

For the next six years Iqbal was chained to a loom in a carpet factory for fourteen hours a day, six days a week.

Iqbal was small and weak. He was repeatedly beaten (*battu*) for disobedience and was given very little food.

When he was ten he escaped and went to school for the first time. He also started to campaign for basic human rights for children in his country, Pakistan.

He became a hero of the anti-slavery movement and visited many countries, including the United States. His message was always the same: "The two hundred million enslaved children in the world are *your* responsibility!"

Iqbal helped to liberate thousands of children but, on Easter Sunday 1995, there was a tragedy. At the age of 12, he was shot and killed while riding his bicycle in his village of Muritke, in Pakistan.

Adapted from Unicef Publications.

## 4 LISTEN

- Check! Right or wrong?
- More about Iqbal.

www.unicefusa.org

# Encore

## 1 REACT

1

2

3

## 2 READ

- Read and answer in your workbook.

## 3 LISTEN

- **Oral comprehension.**
  Ben's timetable in the US.

- **Phonetics and dictation.**
  Hi from San Francisco!

# Oral recap.

- **Say the words aloud!**

**Name five places in your school!**

**Name five school subjects!**

**Name five actions you do in the English lesson!**

- **Give directions!**

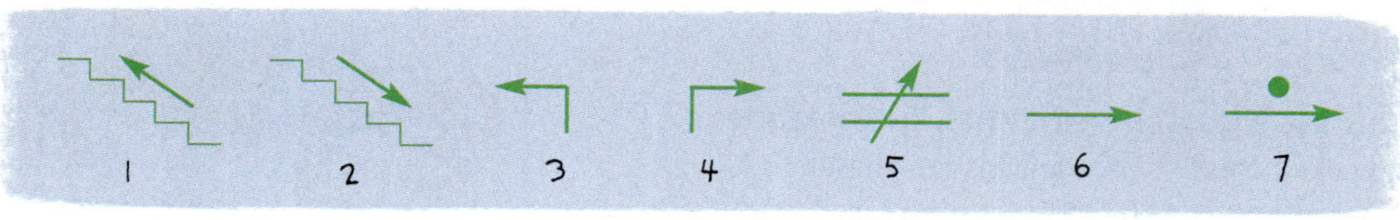


- **Say the words, then spell them aloud!**

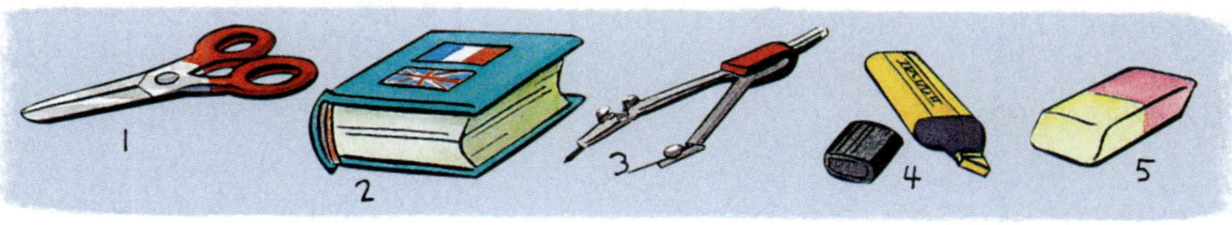


- **Find the odd one out! Then invent a series to read to the class.**

polite - good-tempered - tidy - patient - quiet - lazy
husband - wife - son - daughter - caretaker - mother - father - child
pad - ballpen - pencil - pen - highlighter - paint-brush - colouring pencil

# Word builder

- **Here are the verbs. Who does what?**

teach drive garden
paint clean
act sing farm

Teachers teach.

Teaching is their job.

- **Find the odd one out and explain.**

worker - smoker - helper - writer - learner - organizer - brother - eater - drinker

Form verb to noun:
- verb + -er / -or (teacher, actor) = the person.
- verb + -ing (teaching, acting) = the job / activity.

# Grammar

## NOM + "S" (LE GÉNITIF)

Quand tu sais à qui sont les choses, tu les "attaches" à une personne en utilisant -'s. C'est comme une "ficelle".

Sophie ●———— 's ————● book

Sophie's book.

Le nom du propriétaire vient en premier. C'est le repère.
Le lien marqué par -'s est très fort. A l'oral, ça s'entend !

Sophie's [z] Mike's [s] James's [ɪz]

## WHOSE?

Quand tu ne sais pas à qui sont les choses, tu demandes :

Whose book is this? Whose pens are these?

Ici tu veux relier *book, pens,* etc. à quelqu'un de précis.

⚠ Ne confonds pas :

Who is it? [je cherche l'identité]
Whose house is it? [je cherche le / la propriétaire]

Comment réponds-tu à *Whose book is it?*

## HAVE GOT

| + | ? | – |
|---|---|---|
| I / You have (got). | Have I / you got? | I / You have not got. |
| He / She / It has (got). | Has he / she / it got? | He / She / It has not got. |
| We / You / They have (got). | Have we / you / they got? | We / You / They have not got. |

Poser une question et y répondre :

Have you (got) a dog?
You have (got) a dog, haven't you?
→ Yes, I have.
→ No, I haven't.

## LIKE

*Like* est un verbe lexical (ordinaire). Rappelle-toi :

\+ I, you, we, they like art.
He, she, it likes art.

– I, you, we, they don't like art.
He, she, it doesn't like art.

? Do you like art? Yes, I do. / No, I don't.
Does she like art? Yes, she does. / No, she doesn't.

## ENTRAÎNE-TOI

### Setting the scene

**1 Demande à qui sont ces objets et réponds en t'aidant des initiales.**

### Scene 1

**2 *Be* ou *have* ? Complète.**

1. Mr ICU's daughter ... two years old.
2. She ... got long fair hair.
3. She ... very sweet, ... she?
4. ... Mr ICU got a son? Yes he ... .
5. His name ... Mike. He ... 4.

**3 Retrouve les phrases.**

1. is / brother / friendly / ? / your
2. daughter / Mr ICU / shy / 's / is
3. Mrs Wilson / clumsy / is / 's / husband / ?
4. Mr ICU / are / pupils / lazy / 's
5. aren't / sociable / you / ? / you / , / are

### Scene 2

**4 Dis le contraire en ajoutant ou en supprimant *not*.**

1. I like school.
2. Mr ICU likes lazy pupils.
3. James has forgotten his book today.
4. He hasn't done his exercise.
5. The teacher doesn't want James to listen.

**5 Complète par le verbe *like* à la forme qui convient.**

1. ... you ... music?
2. I ... not ... pop music, but I ... jazz.
3. ... your father ... sport?
4. He ... watching matches on the telly.
5. Mine ... not ... sport. He ... art.

*It's Sophie's (book).* [nom du propriétaire + 's] ou *It's my book* ou *It's mine / yours* [pronoms possessifs]. Le 's de *yours* est le même que dans *Whose?* et *Sophie's*.

# Grammar

MORE!
▶ EXERCISE BANK, P. 162
▶ GRAMMAR STORE, P. 142

## LES PRONOMS PERSONNELS

| sujet | I | you | he | she | it | we | they |
|---|---|---|---|---|---|---|---|
| complément | me | you | him | her | it | us | them |

⚠ Ordre des mots : I like her. She likes them.

## LE PRÉSENT EN *"BE + -ING"*

Le présent en *be + ing* fait entrer dans une situation particulière.

- Observer une scène, décrire ce qui se passe en ce moment !
  Look! The teachers are drinking tea in the staff room.
- Commenter la réalité ["c'est vu, c'est compris !"]
  You're not working! You're cheating! ["je le vois bien que tu triches !"]
- Braquer l'attention sur le sujet ("regardez-le !") et lui attribuer une action ou une attitude : Rob is revising. He is smiling.

| + | ? | − |
|---|---|---|
| I am working.<br>You are working. Etc. | Am I working?<br>Are you working? Etc. | I am not working.<br>You are not working. Etc. |

Si je dis *Rob is reading, isn't he?* que me réponds-tu ?

## LE PRÉSENT SIMPLE

Un message simple : "voilà ce qui est" ou "voilà ce qui se fait".
In Britain, teachers eat, drink and relax in the staff room.

L'important, c'est d'identifier le type d'action (eat? drink? clean?), de sensation (feel?), de sentiment (like? love?). Utile pour :

- établir un fait : Mrs Lunt cleans the school.
- signaler une habitude : She gets up at 6.
- donner une opinion, un sentiment : She likes her job.

Pour poser des questions et y répondre, tu utilises l'auxiliaire *do* :

Does Mrs Lunt work?
Mrs Lunt works, doesn't she?
→ Yes, she does.
→ No, she doesn't.

⚠ Pour indiquer le métier de quelqu'un, n'oublie pas l'article indéfini !
Mr ICU teaches. He is a teacher.

## L'IMPÉRATIF

Cap sur l'action ! Droit au but ! C'est clair, c'est court, ça claque !
Tu nommes directement l'action avec la base verbale (Read!).
Utile pour donner des ordres (Go!) ou donner un itinéraire.

| + | − |
|---|---|
| Turn left! | Don't turn right! |

## ENTRAÎNE-TOI

### Scene 3

**6 Invente des mini-dialogues.**
*Ex.: Look at her. What is she doing?*
*She is ...ing, isn't she?*

**7 Complète par un *tag*.**
1. You are not working, ...?
2. Rob is speaking on the phone, ...?
3. They are not talkative, ...?
4. She has got a dog, ...?
5. Aliette is chatting with Ian, ...?

**8 Voici où ils sont. Imagine ce qu'ils font.**
*I suppose / I imagine ... . Maybe ...*
1. Aliette is in the street.
2. Rob is in the living-room.
3. Sophie is in the bus.
4. The Wilsons are in the kitchen.
5. Mr ICU is in the staff room.

### Scene 4

**9 Établis des faits.**
*Ex.* : Mrs Lunt / school
→ *Mrs Lunt cleans the school, doesn't she? She is a cleaner.*
1. Mr Hopkins / flowers
2. Mrs Collins / school lunches
3. Miss Wade / pupils
4. Mr Kelly / buildings
5. Mr Burton / pupils' parents

**10 Présent simple ou en *be + -ing* ?**
1. Listen! He (sing).
2. He is a singer. He (sing) very well.
3. Where ... he (sing)?
4. He (sing) all around the world.
5. What ... he (sing) now?

Tu réponds *"Yes, he is."* ou *"No, he isn't"*, ou alors *"I don't know"* si tu ne sais pas.

workshop 1

# Do-it-yourself

**Make a calendar! Write in pencil first!**

YOU NEED:
- three round circles of cardboard (120 mm)
- one rectangular sheet of cardboard (175 x 297 mm)
- a pencil
- a cutter
- three pins

**1** ON THE CARDBOARD SHEET, CUT OUT THREE RECTANGLES (45 X 10 MM) AND MAKE THREE HOLES IN THE EXACT POSITIONS SHOWN.

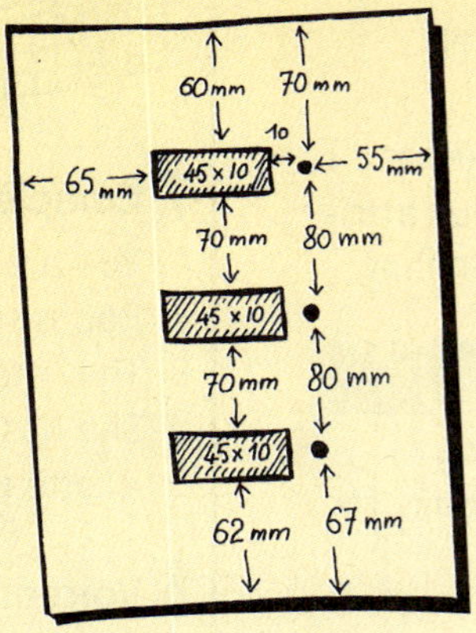


**2** ATTACH THE CIRCLES BEHIND THE CARDBOARD SHEET WITH THE PINS.

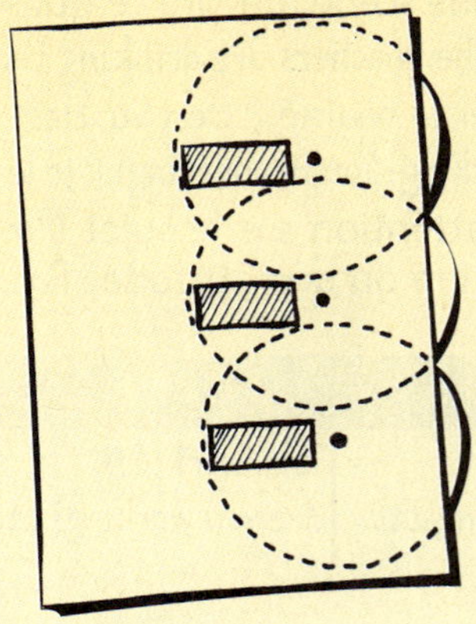

**3** IN THE FIRST RECTANGLE WRITE THE 7 DAYS OF THE WEEK (WRITE «SUNDAY», TURN THE CIRCLE, WRITE «MONDAY», ETC.)

**4** IN THE SECOND RECTANGLE WRITE THE 12 MONTHS OF THE YEAR.

**5** IN THE THIRD RECTANGLE WRITE THE NUMBERS: 1ST, 2ND, 3RD, 4TH, ... 31ST.

**6** DECORATE YOUR CALENDAR, BRING IT TO CLASS AND PRACTISE SAYING DATES.

**Visit the website of an American, British or Canadian school. Present it to your class.**

# Project

## My school!

- Make a file about your school.
  - Age of building(s)?
  - Number of teachers, pupils, classrooms?
  - Languages?
  - Good and bad sides (food, clubs, discipline, etc.)?
- Use pictures and a map.

Choose the best files and exhibit them in the CDI.

## The "I spy" Game

1 One person begins. He looks around the room and selects an object. He mustn't say what it is!

2 He says: "I spy with my little eye, something beginning with 'p'."

3 The other players try to guess the object: "Is it a pen?" "Yes, it is. / No, it isn't."

4 The winner selects the next object.

web site
www.spring.hachette-education.com

# ACT 2

## DANS CE CHAPITRE

### TU VAS T'EXERCER

- à parler de sports.
- à parler de passe-temps.
- à évoquer la vie quotidienne au présent et au passé.
- à parler de personnages historiques.
- à lire pour découvrir la vie des Romains en Grande-Bretagne.

### TU VAS REVOIR

- *"can / can't"*.
- le présent simple avec *"always, often"*, etc.
- le prétérit régulier.

### TU VAS UTILISER

- *"how well? how often?"*
- V + *"-ing"* pour parler d'activités.
- le prétérit irrégulier.

# Life past and present

# Setting the scene

▶ DIS QUELS SPORTS TU PRATIQUES.
▶ PARLE DE L'ÉQUIPEMENT.
▶ ÉVALUE TON NIVEAU.

## Sports

- A penny for your thoughts! Say what you can. Ask questions.

### Swimming

a swimming pool

### Racing

a race track

### Basketball

a court

### Riding

a ring

- Play and learn new words.
- Show you understand. What can Sophie and Kevin do?
- Your turn now!

a. Your talents.

Can you play rugby?

Yes, I can.

How well can you play?

I can't play very well at all.

b. Make riddles.

A: To do this sport, you need a racket and ... B: It is ..., isn't it?

## Cycling / biking

the country

## Baseball

a field

## Football

a pitch

## Rugby

a pitch

## Tennis

a court

## forget-me-not

**Vérifie que tu sais...** - parler de sports et d'équipements sportifs.
- évaluer ton niveau.

Kevin cannot ride at all, can he? He needs lessons.

**Rappelle-toi :** au moins cinq mots nouveaux pour parler de sport.

**"CAN"**

*On sait !*
*On y arrive !*
ə
I can swim.

**"CANNOT"**

*On ne sait pas !*
*On n'y arrive pas !*
I **cannot** swim.

ɑː
can't

**"HOW WELL?"**

++++ very well
++ quite well
+ a little
x not at all

# scene 1

▶ PARLE DE TES PASSE-TEMPS ET DU TEMPS QUE TU Y CONSACRES.
▶ DONNE DES DÉTAILS.

## 1 SHOW YOU KNOW

- **Talk for 15 seconds non-stop: sports in your family.**

## 2 DISCOVER MORE

- **Talk about popular hobbies.**
  A: Many people like gardening.
  B: Some like looking after their pets. Others ...

1

2

3

- **Listen to them. What are their hobbies?** WB

## 3 YOUR TURN NOW!

- **Say your hobby. The class asks questions.**

I love ...ing.

How often do you ...?

How well can you ...?

How many ...?

- **Magic Lingo: The alchemy of "-ing".**

Good gardeners love planting gardenias in their gardens.

## THINK AND STORE

**1** **Read and imagine the scene. Make sure you understand everything!**

**Mr ICU** : What do you do in your spare time, James?
**James** : I enjoy listening to music and acting. I belong to a drama club.
**Mr ICU** : How often does your club meet?
**James** : Once a week. On Friday evenings.

**Mr ICU** : What are your hobbies, Kevin?
**Kevin** : I make models and I also repair things.
**Mr ICU** : So, you're a DIY person. What do you repair?
**Kevin** : Everything. Especially cars.
**Mr ICU** : Cars? Can you really repair cars?
**Kevin** : Yes, I can. I help at Dad's garage twice a week.

**Mr ICU** : Ian, what do you enjoy doing?
**Ian** : Well, surfing the net and collecting spiders.
**Mr ICU** : Yuck! Dead ones, I hope?
**Ian** : Yes, they're dead. But my favourite hobby is looking after my pet, Juliet. *She*'s alive! I walk her three times a day.

### HELP!

spare time: free time

ɪ
en**joy**: like

I be**long** to a club: I am a member.

ʌ
once: one time
twice: two times

DIY: do-it-yourself

e　　əlaɪv
dead ≠ **a**live

**2** **Count all the hobbies. How many have you got?**

**3** **Open your workbook and learn your lesson step by step.**

▶ EXERCISES AND GRAMMAR: PAGE 52.

## forget-me-not

**Vérifie que tu sais...** - parler de tes passe-temps et du temps que tu y consacres.

In his spare time, Ian enjoys looking after Juliet.

### V + "-ing"

*Souvent après* love / like / hate.

*Toujours après* enjoy.

I **enjoy** surf**ing** the net.
↓ (*verbe de goût*)　↓ (V)　↓ (ing)

**Rappelle-toi :** ces passe-temps.

1. gardening.
2. hiking.
3. looking after a pet.
4. cooking.
5. making models.
6. repairing things.
7. surfing the web.
8. collecting things.
9. acting.

# scene 2

- ▶ PARLE DE TA VIE QUOTIDIENNE.
- ▶ QUE FAIS-TU SOUVENT? PARFOIS?
- ▶ PARLE DE TES SENTIMENTS.

## 1 SHOW YOU KNOW

- Ask a friend / your teacher about her / his hobbies.
- Talk for 15 seconds non-stop: hobbies and special talents in your family.

## 2 SPRING INTO ACTION

- Talk about what Kevin does every day. What about you?
- Listen and discover how to talk about Kevin's feelings.
- Mime a feeling. The class says what it is.

**HELP!**

**FEELINGS**

happy ≠ sad / de**pre**ssed

**in**terested ≠ bored

full of **e**nergy ≠ tired

pleased ≠ angry / up**set**

worried / anxious

jealous / envious

- **Listen. What do they feel? When? What about you?**
- **Write about your day and your feelings at different times.**

▶ PLAY AND LEARN IN YOUR WORKBOOK.
▶ EXERCISES AND GRAMMAR: PAGE 52.

## forget-me-not

**Vérifie que tu sais...** - parler de ta vie quotidienne et de tes sentiments.

Sophie often worries. She is a worrier!

**Rappelle-toi :** - ces verbes d'actions quotidiennes.

**In the morning:** I wake up, I get up, I wash, I get dressed, I brush my teeth / my hair, I have breakfast, I make my bed.

**In the evening:** I watch television, I get undressed, I go to bed, I go to sleep.

### LE PRÉSENT SIMPLE

*Donne une info de base, tout simplement !*

*Ce qu'on est / ce qu'on a.*
I'm a happy person.

*Ce qu'on fait d'habitude.*
I get up at 7.30.

*Ce qu'on ressent.*
I feel good. I love life!

### LA FRÉQUENCE

always ● often ◕
sometimes ◑ never ⊗

I (don't) **often** make my bed.
↑ *devant le verbe lexical*

# scene 3

▶ PARLE DE PERSONNAGES HISTORIQUES.
▶ RENSEIGNE-TOI SUR LEUR VIE.

## 1 SHOW YOU KNOW

- **What do you do every day? What are your different feelings?**

## 2 DISCOVER MORE

- **Talk about this website. Ask questions.**
  A: Who is number 2?
  T: Nicephore Niepce.
  C: He was born in ... and died in ...
  D: He invented photography, didn't he?

### The History-for-all website

What did they invent? Discover? Explore? Compose? Write? Paint?
Looking for information? Click on a picture.

**TV Highlights**
**History Quiz**
6pm on the
*History-for-all channel*
today!

**This week's quiz**

Which invention do you consider essential?

- ❑ relativity
- ❑ the camera
- ❑ the electric bulb
- ❑ the printing press
- ❑ the telephone
- ❑ the television
- ❑ photography

Click here for results ❑

- **Listen. Practise saying dates and solve the History Quiz.**

## 3 YOUR TURN NOW!

- **Think of a dead celebrity. The class must guess who it is. (nationality, dates, residence, reasons for celebrity).**

"It's a "he"." — "Was he French?" — "Did he compose music?"

**HELP!**
painter - composer
writer - explorer - inventor
politician - king / queen

- **Magic Lingo: The Time Machine.**

"Did Shakespeare write 'Julius Caesar'?" "Yes, he did." "Who killed Caesar?" "Brutus did."

## THINK AND STORE

**1 Read and imagine the scene. Make sure you understand everything.**

*"The History Quiz" is a TV programme for young people.*

**Sue** : Male or female?
**Host** : Male.
**Ben** : When was he born and where?
**Host** : He was born in 1564 in Stratford-on-Avon, England. He died there in 1616 but he worked in London for many years.
**Sue** : Did he get married? Did he have any children?
**Host** : Yes, he did. He got married and he had three children.

**Ben** : When did he become famous?
**Host** : When he went to London. He wrote plays and acted in them. Even the Queen and the King came to see him.
**Sue** : How many plays did he write?
**Host** : He wrote thirty-eight plays and more than 150 poems.
**Ben** : Did he write "Hamlet" and "Romeo and Juliet" and "Julius Caesar"?
**Host** : Yes he did. So, who is it?

**2 Count all the questions. How many have you found?**

**3 Open your workbook and learn your lesson step by step.**

### HELP!

eɪ ə
**fa**mous

eɪ iː
male ≠ **fe**male

to be born ≠ to die

even: *même*

a play

▶ EXERCISES AND GRAMMAR: PAGE 53.

## forget-me-not

**Vérifie que tu sais...** - parler d'un personnage historique.
- poser des questions sur sa vie.

William Shakespeare was a famous writer, wasn't he?
He wrote lots of plays and poems, didn't he?

**Rappelle-toi :** le prétérit de ces verbes irréguliers.

1. come → came 2. get → got 3. go → went 4. have → had 5. write → wrote

### LE PRÉTÉRIT

*Parler du passé.*

**Verbes réguliers**

**?**
**Did** he live in ...?

**–**
He **did not** live in ... .

**+**
He liv**ed** ... [d]
He work**ed** ... [t]
He act**ed** ... [ɪd]

**"Be"**
I, he / she / it **was**.
We / you / they **were**.

# scene 4

▶ RACONTE AU PASSÉ.
▶ POSE DES QUESTIONS AU PASSÉ.

## 1 SHOW YOU KNOW

- Talk for 15 seconds non-stop about William Shakespeare.
- Play a "History Quiz" with your teacher.

## 2 SPRING INTO ACTION

- Look and say what you can.
- Listen and learn how to talk about Ben's day last Saturday.
- Test your friends' memories.
  A: What time did Ben get up? B: What did he have for ...?

- **What about your last weekend? Ask questions and compare.**

> What time did you get up on Sunday?
>
> I got up at ...

- **Listen: Jim Ricotti's story.**

▶ PLAY AND LEARN IN YOUR WORKBOOK.
▶ EXERCISES AND GRAMMAR: PAGE 53.

**SAY IT!**

| | |
|---|---|
| [eɪt] ate | [bɔːt] bought |
| [dræŋk] drank | [sɔː] saw |
| [spəʊk] spoke | [swæm] swam |
| [tʊk] took | |

## forget-me-not

**Vérifie que tu sais...** - parler du passé.

Yesterday Ben went to the beach, didn't he?
He didn't go to school.

**Rappelle-toi :** - le prétérit de ces verbes irréguliers.

| | | |
|---|---|---|
| 1. buy → bought | 4. get up → got up | 7. speak → spoke |
| 2. drink → drank | 5. see → saw | 8. swim → swam |
| 3. eat → ate | 6. sleep → slept | 9. take → took |

**LE PRÉTÉRIT**
**Verbes irréguliers**

**+**

*Impossible de deviner leur forme.*

I ate, I drank, I swam, etc.

**? –**

*C'est facile !*

**Did** you swim? — Yes, I **did**. / No, I **didn't**.

I **didn't** swim.

# Put pen to paper

## 1 Learn to write better!

Read and correct in your workbook. WB

**Punctuation and capital letters**

my great grandfather was french he came from brittany he was born near brest and he went to america in 1920 do you know what he did there

**Style**

Shakespeare was a great writer.
Shakespeare was a great actor.
Shakespeare was born in 1564.
Shakespeare died in 1616.
Shakespeare wrote a lot of great plays and a lot of great poems.

## 2 Write it yourself!

a. Choose between these two subjects.

**A BIOGRAPHY**
1. A dead celebrity's life.
2. My ancestor's life.

b. Collect the information you need.

Name: ..............................

- date of birth: ..............................
- place of birth: ..............................
- nationality: ..............................
- residence: ..............................
- education: ..............................
- likes and dislikes: ..............................
- married: ☐ yes ☐ no
- number of children: ..............................
- famous for: ..............................
- date of death: ..............................
- place of death: ..............................
- reasons for my choice: ..............................

Need help? Workbook!

c. Write a rough copy of your biography.

d. Can you write better? Check the punctuation and improve the style.

e. Copy out your biography. Be creative!

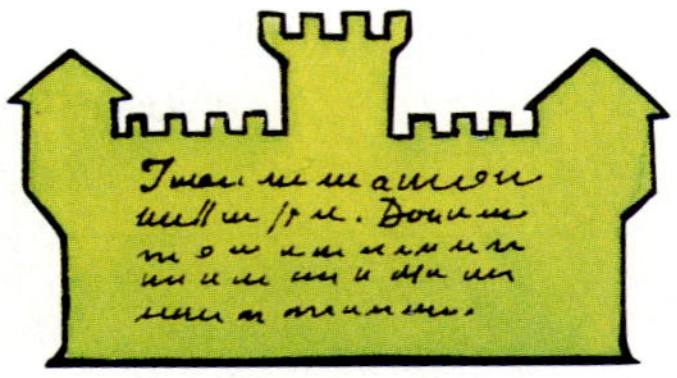

# scene 5

DÉCOUVRE L'ÉPOQUE ROMAINE EN GRANDE-BRETAGNE.
▶ Dis ce que tu sais.
▶ Prépare-toi.
▶ Lis.

# Life in Roman Times

## 1 WHAT DO YOU KNOW? WB

- What do you know about the Roman Empire and Roman Britain?

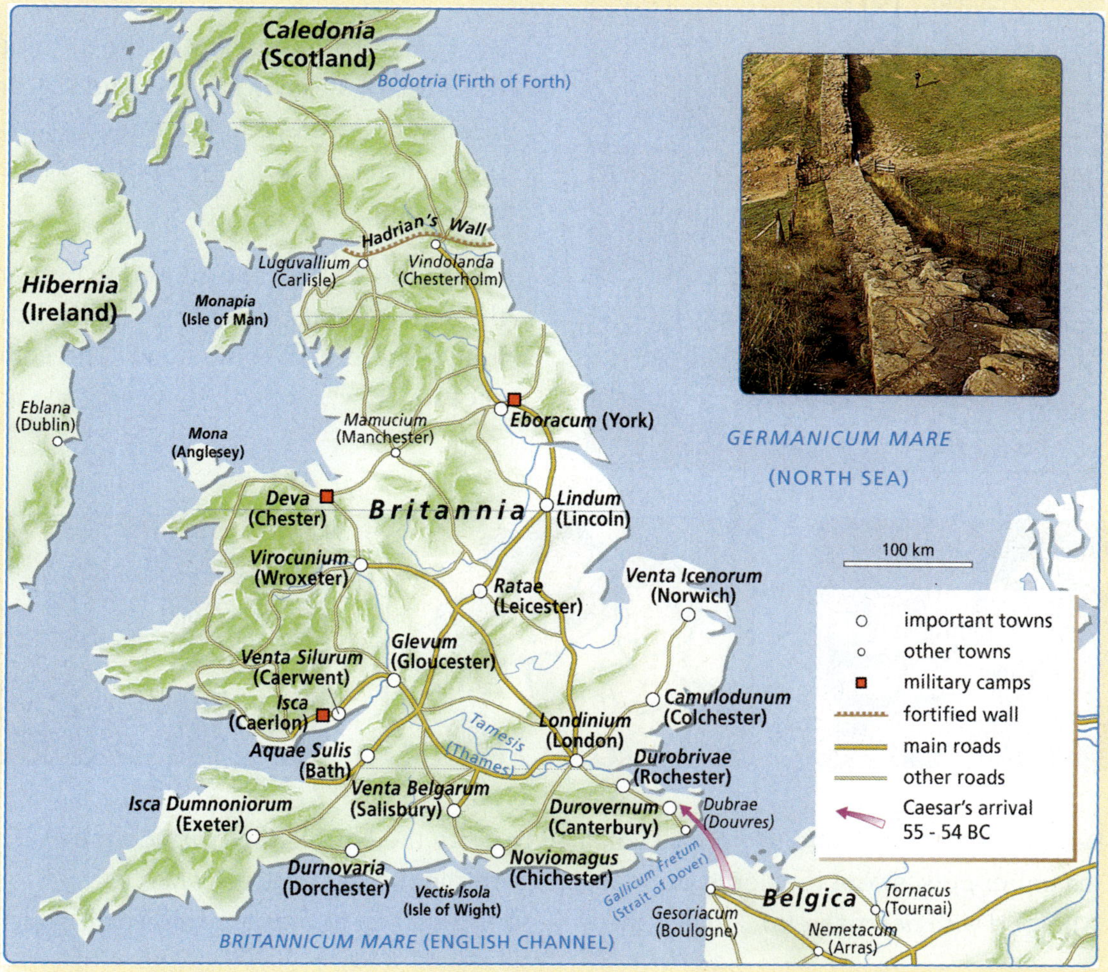


## 2 PREPARE TO READ WB

- **The first text is about Lydia. It includes these words.**

chamber pots    clean, dust and sweep    serve    accompany her mistress

**Lydia is ... a.** a dancer. **b.** the emperor's daughter. **c.** a servant or a slave.

- **The second text is about Felicius. It includes these words.**

the 6th Legion    emperor    garrison    castle    fort    veteran

**Felicius is ... a.** a gladiator. **b.** a soldier. **c.** a senator.

# scene 5

## 3 SPRING INTO ENGLISH

- **Reading strategies: the numbers, dates and times of day will help you. Spot them!**

Lydia lived in Londinium. She was a slave in the household of Paulus. In 125 AD she was twelve years old. She spoke Latin, of course, but she couldn't read or write.

1

Every day Lydia got up at the 1st hour, which was 4.30 am in summer and 7.30 am in winter. She slept in her tunic because the Romans did not have special clothes to sleep in.

During the 2nd hour she helped to prepare the family's *ientaculum*. They had a little fruit, some bread, some honey and some cheese.

2

3

4

During the 3rd, 4th, 5th and 6th hours, Lydia had to clean the house. She emptied the chamber pots, swept the floors and dusted. Then she did her mistress's hair and helped with her make-up. Finally, she went to the kitchen to prepare *prandium*.

5

Lydia sometimes accompanied her mistress to the public baths, where the Romans washed but also met their friends and socialized.
In the evening there was often a big feast: *cena*. Lydia helped to serve the food and drink, and sometimes she played the harp.

# Felicius, a soldier in Britannia in 130 AD.

Ave! My name is Felicius. I belong to the 6th Legion stationed at Eburacum. I was born in Iberia 45 years ago and I joined the Roman Legion 23 years ago.
I came to Britannia with Emperor Hadrian to build a wall to mark the northern limit of our Empire.
We finished it 4 years ago. It is about 80 miles long, 20 feet high and 10 feet thick. Every mile there is a little castle for a garrison of 25 soldiers, and there are some bigger forts too.
Many of us come from the south and hate the cold weather here.
Luckily we have warm socks and special clothes to keep us warm.
To improve our morale, we are now allowed to get married and so we have women and children in our forts.
In two years' time I am going to retire and I hope to live the rest of my life with my family here in Britannia, on land Rome gives its veterans.

## 4 LISTEN

- Check! Right or wrong?
- Britain after the Romans.

www.vindolanda.com

# Encore

## 1 REACT

- **Say what you can or ask questions (name, dates, residence, family, etc.).**

1

742-814

2

1452-1519

3

1533-1603

4

1564-1616

5

1769-1821

6

1881-1973

7

1935-1977

8

1961-1997

## 2 READ

- **Read and find out who it is.**

He was an energetic, intelligent, hard-working and courageous ruler. But he was also tyrannical and sometimes cruel.
He wanted to reconstruct the Roman Empire and conquered many lands in Italy, France and Germany.
He spoke German, Latin, and understood Greek. He was interested in philosophy and religion and was a great protector of the arts. He re-organised schools, but he didn't invent them. Some people say he didn't know how to write. But at that time, writing was a difficult art called calligraphy and only a few educated people practised it.

## 3 LISTEN

- **Oral comprehension.**
More about the mystery person.

- **Phonetics and dictation.**
An emperor's daily life.

# Oral recap.

- **Say the words aloud!**

**Name six sports!**

**Name six things you do every morning!**

**Name six actions you did last weekend!**

- **Say if you enjoy these hobbies or not.**

I enjoy ... but
I don't like ...

- **Find the odd one out! Then invent a series for the class.**

sad - anxious - worried - pleased - unhappy - upset - depressed
jump - shorts - ball - court - basket - jersey - dribble - pedal
wrote - drank - went - slept - saw - spoke - eat - came

# Word builder

- **Make as many compound nouns as you can. Then make sentences.**

skate basket tennis roller
team ball table foot net
bat court
board racket base score

A tennis racket

I play tennis with a tennis racket.

- **Now find the compound nouns.**

1. It is a suit you swim in.
2. They are shoes you wear for running.
3. It is a hat you wear for riding.
4. It is a helmet you wear when you ride a bike.

- **Look at the school things on pages 14-15. How many compound words can you say?**

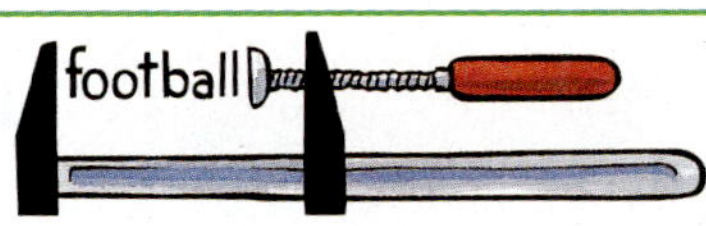


IN ENGLISH YOU OFTEN GLUE WORDS TOGETHER! THEY ARE CALLED COMPOUND WORDS.

# Grammar

## CAN

| On sait le faire ! On y arrive ! ⊕ | Est-ce qu'on sait le faire ? Est-ce qu'on y arrive ? ? | On ne sait pas ! On n'y arrive pas ! ⊖ |
|---|---|---|
| I<br>You can swim. Etc. (ə)<br>He | I<br>Can you swim? Etc.<br>he | I<br>You can't swim. Etc. (ɑː)<br>He |
| En milieu de phrase *can* est inaccentué. | | *Can't* est toujours accentué. |

⚠ Pour répondre à une question avec *can* :

Can she ride? / She can ride, can't she? → Yes, she can. / No, she can't.

*Can't* est une forme contractée. Quelle est la forme pleine ?

## HOW WELL?

Pour te renseigner sur les performances de quelqu'un :

How well can you ski?
- I can ski very well. +++++++
- I can ski quite well. ++++
- I can ski a little. ++
- I can't ski at all. X

## HOW OFTEN?

Pour te renseigner sur la fréquence :

How often do you go to the club?
- Once a week.
- Twice a week.
- Three times a week.

always — often — sometimes — never

⚠ Devant le verbe lexical : I often make my bed. I don't often go shopping.
Après *"be"* : I am often jealous.

## V1 (sentiment / attitude) + V2 + *-ing*

Ian enjoys surf[ing] the net.
V1 V2

V1 : plan du sentiment (enjoy, love, like, hate, prefer) porte la marque du temps (présent, passé)

V2 : plan de l'action (surf, listen), porte le marqueur *-ing*

Avec *-ing*, le verbe et les compléments forment un bloc de sens et occupent la place d'un nom.

I like { computers. / surfing the net.

# ENTRAÎNE-TOI

## Setting the scene

**1 Parle des performances de chacun.**

*Ex. : I can ... very well. / I can't ... at all.*

1. You / 
2. Your best friend / 
3. Your father / 
4. Your gym teacher / 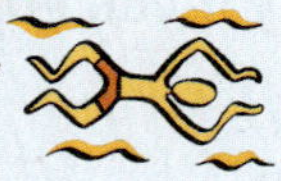
5. You / 

## Scene 1

**2 *How often* ou *how well* ? Complète et réponds.**

1. ... can you ski?
2. ... do you go skiing?
3. ... do your parents give you presents?
4. ... does your mother cook?
5. ... do you play tennis?

**3 Réponds en donnant des précisions sur les performances.**

*Ex. :* Do you like swimming?
*Yes, I do, but I can't swim very well.*

1. Do you like horse riding?
2. Does your father like cycling?
3. Does your mother enjoy gardening?
4. Do you enjoy repairing things?
5. Does anyone in your family enjoy cooking?

## Scene 2

**4 Retrouve les questions et réponds.**

1. bed / often / make / your / do / you / ?
2. feel / do / sometimes / you / depressed / ?
3. Ian / how / does / walk / Juliet / often / ?
4. you / like / do / rap / to / listening / ?
5. does / feel / Kevin / when / jealous / ?

**5 Dis-le en anglais.**

1. Ta mère te demande si tu peux l'aider.
2. Tu réponds que tu ne peux pas. Tu es occupé(e).
3. Elle te demande ce que tu fais.
4. Tu réponds que tu répares ton vélo.
5. Elle te rappelle que tu ne l'aide jamais.

La forme pleine qui correspond à la forme contractée *can't* est *cannot*, en un seul mot.

# Grammar

MORE!
▶ EXERCISE BANK, P. 164
▶ GRAMMAR STORE, P. 142

## LE PRÉTÉRIT

Tu remontes dans le temps, tu t'intéresses au passé, tu racontes.

| + | ? | − |
|---|---|---|
| I<br>You worked. | Did I<br>you work? | I<br>You did not work. |
| He<br>She worked.<br>It | he<br>Did she work?<br>it | He<br>She did not work.<br>It |
| We<br>You worked.<br>They | we<br>Did you work?<br>they | We<br>You did not work.<br>They |

*-ed* signale une coupure avec la réalité du moment présent.
Quand on "coupe", ça laisse une marque *(-ed)*, ça produit un son :
worked [t] composed [d] acted [ɪd]

Pour poser une question sur le passé et y répondre :

Did Shakespeare marry?
Shakespeare married, didn't he?
→ Yes, he did.
→ No, he didn't.

Observe bien le tableau.
**+** Combien y a-t-il de formes pour le verbe lexical ?
**? −** Quel auxiliaire utilises-tu ?

## LES VERBES IRRÉGULIERS

Ne suivent pas la règle de fabrication normale : base verbale + *-ed*.
On ne peut pas deviner leur forme affirmative **+**.

| | | | | | |
|---|---|---|---|---|---|
| be | → | was (sing.) were (plur.) | have | → | had |
| buy | → | bought | see | → | saw |
| come | → | came | sleep | → | slept |
| do | → | did | speak | → | spoke |
| drink | → | drank | swim | → | swam |
| eat | → | ate | steal | → | stole |
| go | → | went | take | → | took |
| get | → | got | write | → | wrote |

## WHEN ...?

Situer un événement dans le temps.
Utile pour rechercher *(wh-?)* la date ou le lieu de naissance :

When [were] you born? I was born in 1991.
When [was] he born? He was born in 1564.

La naissance appartient au passé. Le verbe est donc au prétérit.

## ENTRAÎNE-TOI

### Scene 3

**6 Complète par un verbe au prétérit et ajoute un *tag*.**

1. Mozart ... beautiful music, ...?
2. Bell ... the telephone, ...?
3. Dickens ... a writer, ...?
4. Raphael ... portraits, ...?
5. Einstein ... in 1955, ...?

**7 Dis le contraire en utilisant ou en supprimant *not*.**

1. Shakespeare was born in Ireland.
2. He lived in Dublin.
3. He didn't work in London.
4. He didn't write poems.
5. The Queen didn't often come to see him.

### Scene 4

**8 Pose la question qui convient.**

1. James and Ian went to xxx.
2. They saw *"Star Wars"* last xxx.
3. Ian's parents bought him a xxx.
4. I drank xxx for breakfast.
5. Yesterday I ate xxx.

**9 Exprime ton désaccord.**

*Ex. :* Kevin went to Chicago last year.
→ *No, he **didn't go** to Chicago.
He **went** to New York.*

1. Mr ICU took his daughter to the circus.
2. The champion swam 100 m in 55".
3. The children bought their mother a bag.
4. The campers slept for eight hours.
5. We saw *"Hamlet"* at Christmas.

**10 a. Dis-le en anglais.**

1. Dickens écrivit *"Oliver Twist"* en 1838.
2. Ricotti a volé une voiture l'an dernier.
3. Tu es allé(e) en Angleterre en août.
4. Tu n'es pas né(e) à Londres.

**b. Demande à un camarade ...**

5. où il est né.
6. quand il a vu le film *"Romeo et Juliet"*.

**+** : une seule forme, quelle que soit la personne ! Il suffit de fixer *-ed* à la base verbale *(worked)*. Facile !
**? −** : on utilise l'auxiliaire *did* qui est le prétérit de *do*. Cette forme, irrégulière, est la même pour toutes les personnes.
Toujours aussi facile !

# Do-it-yourself

## Make a bedroom-door poster!

YOU NEED:
- a poster
- cardboard or thick drawing paper
- crayons or paint
- scissors
- string

**1** USING THICK PAPER, DRAW AND CUT OUT SHAPES AS IN THE DRAWING.

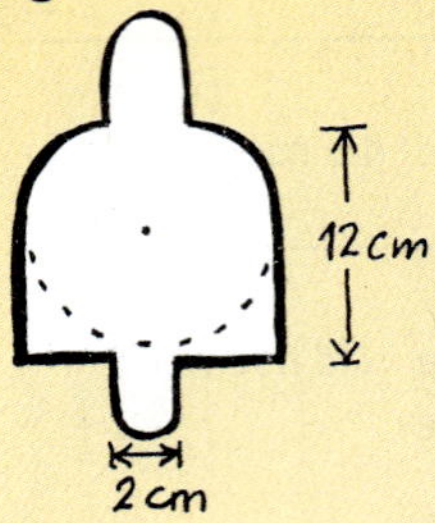


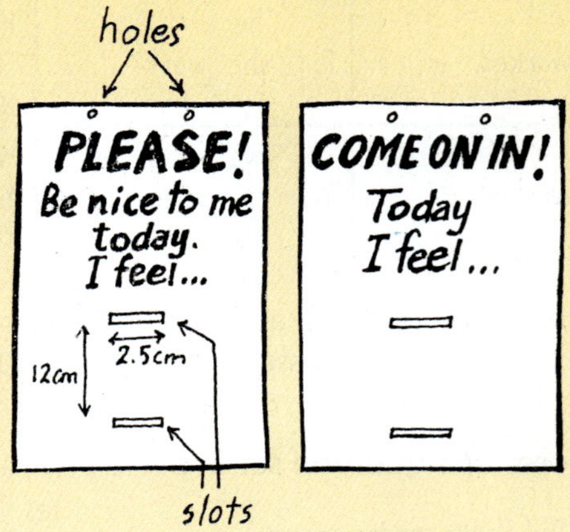


**2** PREPARE THE POSTER. MAKE TWO HOLES AT THE TOP AND TWO SLOTS, AS IN THE DRAWING.

**3** WRITE A POSITIVE GREETING ON ONE SIDE AND A NEGATIVE GREETING ON THE OTHER.

**4** DRAW YOUR FEELINGS AND WRITE THE WORD.

**5** SHOW IT TO THE CLASS AND THEN HANG IT ON YOUR BEDROOM DOOR.

Find out more about Shakespeare or Stratford-on-Avon.

# Project

## Make a town history album

YOU NEED: - photos or postcards of buildings in your town
- Bristol cards with holes
- pens or markers
- scissors, string and glue.

- Find information about a building or monument in your town.
  - Who built it?
  - When? What for?
  - Characteristics?
- Glue the photo or postcard onto a Bristol card.
- Write about the building on the back.
- Bring the card to school and make a class album!

Why not send your history album to your penfriends?

## The trivia question game

1 Use an encyclopedia, the internet or magazines to learn about a famous person or invention.

2 Choose five facts and write out five corresponding questions.

3 On a card, write the name of the famous person or invention at the top, like a title. Then copy the questions and write "Q" in the top corner.

4 On the other side, copy the answers and write "A" in the corner.

5 Combine all the cards to make a trivia game.

A
1. 1917
2. 1963

Q
**John F. Kennedy**
1. When was he born?
2. When did he die?
a) 1889 b) 1963
c) 1989 d) 1998
3. What was his wife's name?
4. How many times was he elected president?
5. What animal was his pet?

web site
www.spring.hachette-education.com

# ACT 3

## DANS CE CHAPITRE

### TU VAS T'EXERCER

- à parler de nourriture.
- à parler d'obligations au présent et au passé.
- à raconter au passé.
- à dire ce qu'il a été possible de faire ou non.
- à donner des conseils.
- à lire pour découvrir le scoutisme.

### TU VAS UTILISER

- *"have to / don't have to".*
- *"had to / didn't have to / couldn't".*
- *"should / shouldn't / mustn't".*
- *"not ... enough / too ...".*

### TU VAS REVOIR

- *"some"* et *"any".*
- *"there is / there are".*
- le présent simple.
- le prétérit.

# Be prepared!

# Setting the scene

- PARLE DE NOURRITURE.
- EXPRIME TES GOÛTS.

## Food

- **A penny for your thoughts! Say what you like / don't like and ask questions.**

- **Play and learn new words.**
- **Show you understand: complete Aliette's shopping list.**
- **Your turn now!**

**a. Play shop. Follow your teacher's instructions.**

Have you got any butter?

No, I haven't got any. ou Yes, I've got some. How much do you want?

**b. Talk about your preferences. Give reasons.**

A: I often eat apples because they are healthy.
B: I had sausages for lunch. I didn't like them because they were greasy.

**HELP!**

**Good for you**
healthy

**Bad for you**
greasy / fatty
full of sugar

**Tasty**
crunchy - juicy
sweet ≠ sour
salty
hot

## forget-me-not

**Vérifie que tu sais...** - parler de tes goûts en nourriture.
- faire des courses.

She bought some organic apples, didn't she?

**Rappelle-toi :** au moins cinq mots nouveaux pour parler d'aliments.

### "SOME"

*Il y en a. C'est sûr !*
There are **some** apples.

*On m'en propose.*
Do you want **some**?

### "ANY"

*Je ne sais pas s'il y en a.*
*Je me renseigne.*
Are there **any** apples?

*Il n'y en a pas. C'est sûr !*
There are**n't any**.

# scene 1

▶ PARLE DE TÂCHES MÉNAGÈRES.
▶ DIS CE QUE TU DOIS FAIRE OU NON.

## 1 SHOW YOU KNOW

- **Food in your family: likes / dislikes? Who eats what? How often? Why?**

## 2 DISCOVER MORE

- **Look and say what you can. Ask questions.**

- **Listen: what are Sophie's chores at camp?**

## 3 YOUR TURN NOW!

- **Chores in your family. Who has to do what?**

I have to make my bed. Do you?

No, I don't.

So who does it?

My Mum does.

- **Conclude.** I have to ... but X doesn't (have to). Her Mum does it.
- **Magic Lingo: No choice!**

HELP!

*I'm awfully sorry, but I can't help you now. I have to work.*

## THINK AND STORE

**1 Read and imagine the scene. Make sure you understand everything.**

**Mrs Macguire** : Hello darling. How are you? Are you enjoying yourself?
**Sophie** : Yes, we're having lots of fun. It's brilliant!
**Mrs Macguire** : Tell me what you do every day.
**Sophie** : Well, we get up at seven. Then we have to tidy our tents and get dressed straight away.
**Mrs Macguire** : I hope you get washed too!
**Sophie** : Of course! And after breakfast we all have different chores.
**Mrs Macguire** : What are yours?
**Sophie** : Well, I have to do the shopping, peel the vegetables and light the fire. After lunch I have to clear the table and do the washing up.
**Mrs Macguire** : You! Peel the veg, wash up! I can't believe it! And who does the cooking? I hope it's not you!
**Sophie** : No, I don't have to cook.
**Mrs Macguire** : Thank goodness for that!

**2 Count the chores. How many have you found?**

**3 Open your workbook and learn your lesson step by step.**

### HELP!

eɪ
straight away: immediately

tʃ
a chore: *une corvée*

aɪ
light the fire

lay / clear the table

I **can't believe** it: It's not possible!

thank goodness: *dieu merci!*

▶ EXERCISES AND GRAMMAR: PAGE 74.

## forget-me-not

**Vérifie que tu sais...** - parler de ce que tu dois faire, de ce que tu n'as pas besoin de faire.

She has to do the shopping, doesn't she?
She doesn't have to cook, does she?

**"HAVE TO"**

*Enchaîne à l'action !*
*Il le faut !*
I **have to** cook.

**"DON'T HAVE TO"**

*Libère de l'action !*
*Pas besoin !*
I **don't have to** cook!

**?**

**Do** you **have to** ... ?
Yes, I **do**. / No, I **don't**.

**Rappelle-toi :** ces tâches ménagères.

1. I tidy up.
2. I sweep the floor.
3. I peel the vegetables.
4. I wash up.
5. I iron.
6. I make my bed.
7. I do the shopping.
8. I hoover.
9. I lay ≠ clear the table.
10. I dust.

# scene 2

▶ PARLE D'OBLIGATIONS PASSÉES : DIS CE QUE TU AS DÛ FAIRE OU NON.

## 1 SHOW YOU KNOW

- Talk about Sophie's chores at camp and about her mother's reactions.
- Interview your teacher about her / his chores at home.

## 2 SPRING INTO ACTION

- Look and say what you can. Ask questions.
- Listen and discover what they had to do to get their badges.

House Orderly Badge

Sally

DIY Badge

Charles

Cyclist Badge

Bill

Gardener Badge

Charlotte

- **Here are Aliette's badges. Imagine what she had to do to get them.**
  A: To get the ... badge, I suppose she had to ...

- **Listen: The Collector's Badge.**
- **Guess my badge! Ask me what I had / didn't have to do to get it.**
- **Write about what you had to do / didn't have to do yesterday.**

▶ PLAY AND LEARN IN YOUR WORKBOOK.
▶ EXERCISES AND GRAMMAR: PAGE 74.

## SAY IT!

ɪz
**bad**ges

**gard**e̸ner

ə
**order**l̸y

ə'dʒɪlɪtɪ
a**gil**ity

ə
col**lec**tor

## forget-me-not

**Vérifie que tu sais...** - parler de ce que tu as dû faire ou non.
- interroger tes camarades à ce sujet.

To get her Cook Badge, Aliette had to make lunch.
But she didn't have to wash up, did she?

**"HAD TO"**

*On a dû le faire.*
*Il le fallait !*
**Yesterday,** I **had to** cook.

**"DIDN'T HAVE TO"**

*Pas besoin !*
*Ce n'était pas nécessaire !*
I **didn't have to** cook.

**?**

**Did** you **have to** ...?
Yes, I **did**. / No, I **didn't**.

**Rappelle-toi :** ces noms.
an **ath**lete - a col**lec**tor - a cook - a **cy**clist
a do-it-your**self** (DIY) person - a film lover - a **gar**dener

# scene 3

▶ RACONTE AU PASSÉ.
▶ POSSIBLE ? IMPOSSIBLE ?
▶ TROP ? PAS ASSEZ ?

## 1 SHOW YOU KNOW

- Talk about Aliette's badges.
- Talk non-stop for 20 seconds about what you had / didn't have to do yesterday.

## 2 DISCOVER MORE

- Look and say what you can about last week's picnic. Ask questions.

- Read or listen to Sophie's e-mail. What happened?

## 3 YOUR TURN NOW!

- Listen and react. What is their problem?

Yuck!

She doesn't like it. Maybe it's too salty.

Or not salty enough.

- Magic Lingo: Excess baggage.

The fish wasn't fresh enough! The chips were too salty! We couldn't eat anything!

## THINK AND STORE

**1** **Read Sophie's e-mail.**

**Subject: picnic**
**From:** Sophie <smacguire@irenet.com>
**To:** Ben <badams@sannet.com>

Hello Ben!
Last weekend we went on a picnic and tried to make pancakes on a camp fire. But everything went wrong!

First Rob didn't manage to light the fire. There was too much wind, it was too wet and he didn't have enough matches. Then we made the batter for the pancakes but it wasn't liquid enough. There wasn't any milk so we had to use water.

After that we realized we didn't have enough sugar. Luckily we found a jar of honey but I couldn't open it. Mark tried, but he couldn't open it either. Everybody tried, but nobody managed. So we had to break it open. And of course it broke into a thousand pieces!

In the end we only got one pancake each, but they were disgusting. On top of everything, it started raining cats and dogs! So Mark took us to the local McDonald's

**HELP!**

ɪdʒ
He didn't manage: he couldn't

wind

wet ≠ dry

ɪˈnʌf
**enough**

ɪz
matches

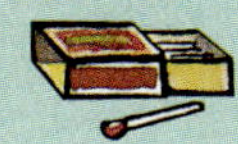

break, broke,

broken

**2** **How many irregular verbs are there? Count them.**

**3** **Open your workbook and learn your lesson step by step.**

▶ EXERCISES AND GRAMMAR: PAGE 75.

## forget-me-not

**Vérifie que tu sais...** - raconter ce qu'il a été possible de faire ou non.
- dire que c'est "trop" ou "pas assez".

He couldn't light the fire! There was too much wind.

**TROP !**

**Too** wet!
*adjectif*

**Too much** wind!
*nom sing.*

**Too many** clouds!
*nom pluriel*

**PAS ASSEZ !**

**Not** warm **enough**!
*adjectif*

**Not enough** sun!
*nom*

**Rappelle-toi :** ces six verbes irréguliers.

1. break → broke
2. find → found
3. get → got
4. go → went
5. make → made
6. take → took

# scene 4

▶ PARLE DU CODE DE LA ROUTE.
▶ DIS CE QUI EST INTERDIT, OBLIGATOIRE, CONSEILLÉ.

## 1 SHOW YOU KNOW

- Talk about the picnic and its problems.
- Relate a recent picnic, meal or party (place, company, food).

## 2 SPRING INTO ACTION

- Look and say what you can.
- Listen and learn how to talk about the highway code.

### What you must not do

1. maximum speed

2. no overtaking

3. no cycling

4. no entry

### What you must do

5. ahead only

6. turn left

7. turn right

8. minimum speed

### Warning signs: you should be careful and slow down

9. crossroads

10. roundabout

11. roadworks ahead

12. elderly people

13. pedestrian crossing

14. school

15. cattle

## Direction and information signs

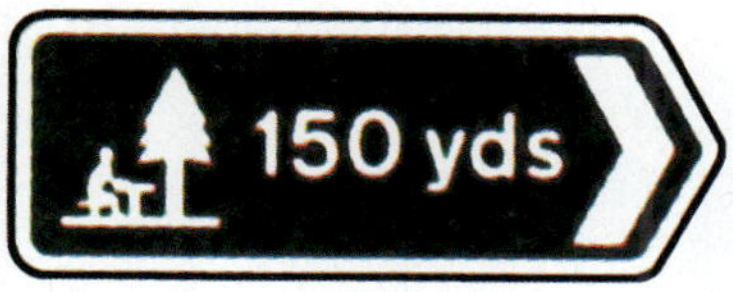

16. picnic site

17. start of motorway

18. end of motorway

- **Listen, draw and answer.**
- **Describe a sign. The class must say the number.**
- **Listen and give them advice. Then give advice to the class.**

**SAY IT!**

aɪ
**hig**hway
e
a**head**
ɔː
**warn**ing
aɪ
sign
aʊ ə aʊ
**round**about
pe**des**trian
**mo**torway
di**rec**tion
ə
infor**ma**tion

▶ PLAY AND LEARN IN YOUR WORKBOOK.
▶ EXERCISES AND GRAMMAR: PAGE 75.

## forget-me-not

**Vérifie que tu sais...** - parler du code de la route.
- dire ce qui est interdit, obligatoire, conseillé.

He's driving too fast. He should slow down, shouldn't he?

**"SHOULD"**
*C'est conseillé !*
You **should** be careful.

*C'est déconseillé !*
You **shouldn't** go so fast.

**"MUSTN'T"**
*À éviter absolument !*
You **mustn't** overtake!
It's dangerous!

**Rappelle-toi :**

THE HIGHWAY CODE

Red circles say what you **must not** do.
Blue circles say what you **must / have to** do.
Warning signs say what you **should** do.
Direction signs give you useful information.

# Put pen to paper

## 1 Learn to write better!

**Read and correct the pupils' mistakes.** WB

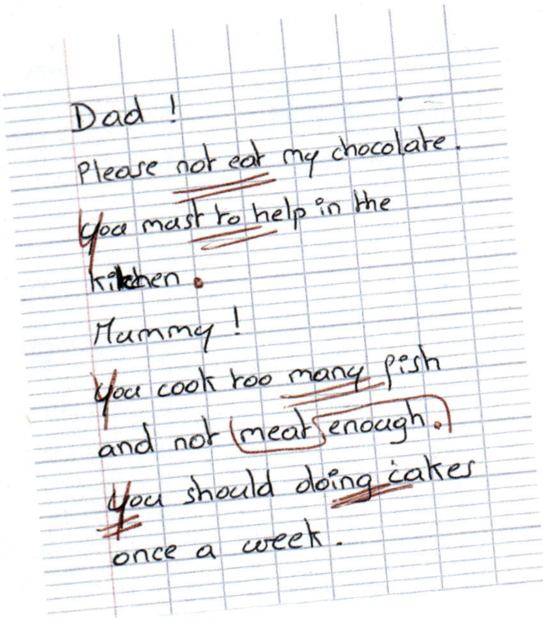
Dad !
Please not eat my chocolate.
You mast to help in the kitchen.
Mummy !
You cook too many fish
and not meat enough.
You should doing cakes
once a week.

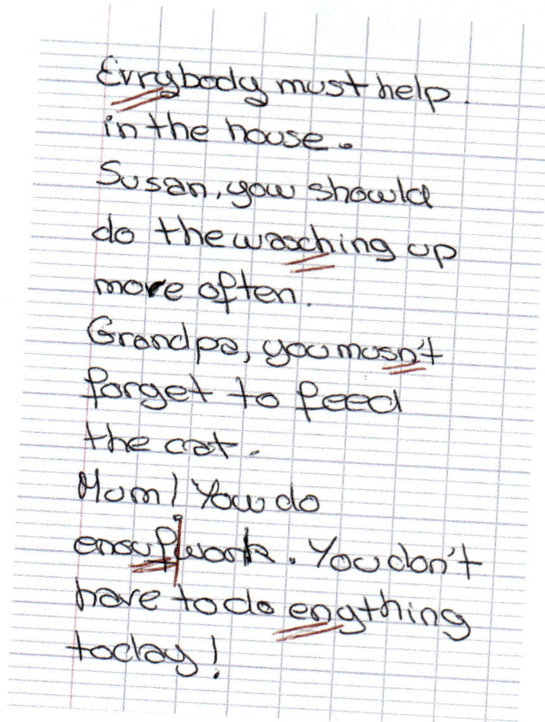
Evrybody must help
in the house.
Susan, you should
do the wasching up
more often.
Grandpa, you musn't
forget to feed
the cat.
Mum! You do
enouf work. You don't
have to do enything
today!

## 2 Write it yourself! WB

**a. Choose one of these codes to put on the fridge door.**

**A FAMILY CODE**
1. a code for food
2. a code for chores

Need help? Workbook!

**b. Write a rough copy.**
- Problems?
- What everybody should / shouldn't do.
- Rules and advice.

**c. Can you write better? Improve your English and your style.**

**d. Copy out your code on a card.**

**e. Decorate it and put it on the fridge door.**

# scene 5

DÉCOUVRE LE SCOUTISME.
▶ Dis ce que tu sais.
▶ Prépare-toi.
▶ Lis.

# Scouting

## 1 WHAT DO YOU KNOW?

- **Say what you know about the Scout movement.**

1

2

3

ONE MOVEMENT!
SOMETHING FOR EVERY AGE!

| ♀ | AGE | ♂ |
|---|---|---|
| A Brownie | 7+ | A Cub |
| A Guide | 10+ | A Scout |
| A Senior Guide | 14+ | A Venture Scout |

## 2 PREPARE TO READ

- **Which of these words may *not* be in the Scout Code of Honour? Why?**

promise honour duty *(devoir)* help aggressive friendly
lazy respect courage hate loyal law *(loi)*

- **"Scout" can be translated as *éclaireur*, so originally a scout was a person who ...**

**a.** was very good at repairing electricity.
**b.** got information about the position of an enemy army.
**c.** loved helping other people.

**Conclude:** The founder of the Scout movement was probably:
**a.** an electrician. **b.** a soldier. **c.** a doctor.

# scene 5

## 3 SPRING INTO ENGLISH

- **Reading strategies: transparent words can help you! Pick them out.**

### The Scout Promise

On my honour I promise that I will do my best
To do my duty to God and to Queen.
To help other people
And to keep the Scout law.

### The salute

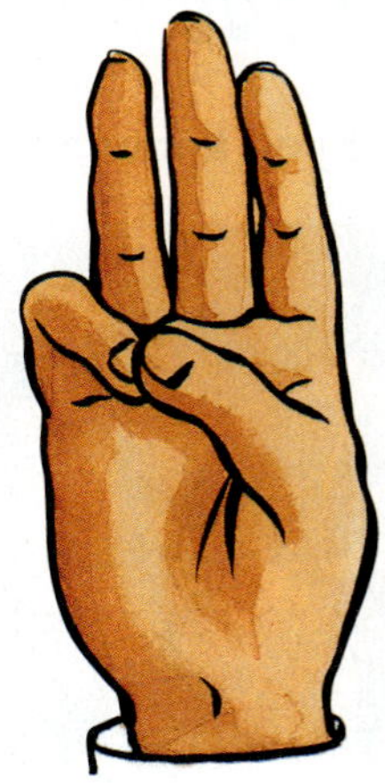

### The motto

BE PREPARED!

### The Millennium Logo

### The Scout Law

A Scout is to be trusted.
A Scout is loyal.
A Scout is friendly and considerate.
A Scout is a brother to all Scouts.
A Scout has courage in difficulties.
A Scout makes good use of his time
And is careful of possessions and property.
A Scout has self-respect and respect for others.

### Uniforms

What differences can you see?

1910

2001

# "BP": a successful founder

## An active child

When Robert Baden Powell was a young boy, he enjoyed playing Indians and pretending he was a hunter or a scout.
With his older brothers, he went on all sorts of expeditions.
They bought old boats and explored the coasts of Britain. They also went on long walks with packs on their backs.

## A soldier

As a young man, Baden Powell became a soldier.
He fought in Africa in 1888 and he acted as a "scout" for the army. He had to find his way in the desert and survive in dangerous situations.
His talents won him the nickname of "*The wolf that never sleeps*".

1857-1941 1889-1977

## A successful founder

When he left the army in 1907, he organized a camp for twenty boys in the south of England. In 1908 he published a book called "*Scouting for boys*".
Two years later there were 100,000 boy scouts in Britain!
Girls soon wanted to join the movement and in 1910 they forced Baden Powell, whose nickname was now BP, to create the *Girl Guide Movement*, in which his wife, Lady Baden Powell, played an important part.
The scouting movement soon became international. In 1922 there were already over one million scouts across the world and today there are 28 million scouts and guides, of all religions and cultures.

## 4 LISTEN

- **Check! Right or wrong?**
- **More about the Scouts.**

**www.scoutbase.org.uk**

# Encore

## 1 REACT

## 2 READ

- **Read and compare with the photos. Highlight the errors in your workbook.**

**1.** This photo was taken in England. There is an enormous traffic jam on a small country road and drivers have to be patient to avoid road rage. Some may be listening to their radios, and others are probably using their mobile phones, but they shouldn't because telephoning in cars is only allowed if you have a hands-free set.

**2.** This child is about 14 years old. He is having a driving lesson in his father's new sports car. He looks worried because he doesn't know his highway code properly.

**3.** This is a Mexican bus which is crossing the boarder into California. It is very crowded and there isn't enough room for everybody. It is so full that some people even have to sit on the roof. They are warmly dressed in winter clothes because the weather is cold and windy.

## 3 LISTEN

- **Oral comprehension.**
  **Identify the pictures. Give advice.**

- **Phonetics and dictation.**
  Rob's cousin in India.

# Oral recap.

- **How many kinds of food can you name for each category?**

for breakfast

for a picnic

mixed salad

- **Say the words.**

- **Say the words and spell them aloud!**

- **Find the odd one out and then invent a series to read to the class.**

greasy - fatty - tasty - salty - crunchy - windy - juicy - healthy
cooking - ironing - dusting - swimming - hoovering - washing-up
drive - turn left - turn right - go straight ahead - overtake - look after - slow down

# Word builder

- **Add the suffix "-y" to make adjectives from these nouns. Then put them in sentences.**

**Food**
sugar - salt - health - juice
crunch - taste - grease - water

**The weather**
sun - rain - wind - cloud - snow

Salty!

I don't like salty food.

- **Find the odd one out and explain.**

tasty - watery - messy - funny - dirty - city - lucky

NOUN + Y → ADJECTIVE

# Grammar

## SOME & ANY

*Some* et *any* indiquent une quantité sans la préciser.

• **SOME** (+) (?) existence certaine ou attendue.
Avec *some* tu t'installes tout de suite dans le réel.
C'est comme si tu voyais ou tenais (déjà) la chose !

| + Il y en a, c'est sûr. ? | |
|---|---|
| Tu le dis.<br>There is some coffee. | Tu en proposes.<br>Do you want some coffee?<br>Tu en demandes.<br>Can I have some sugar? |

• **ANY** (?) existence incertaine. (–) absence.
Avec *any*, tu explores le réel.
C'est comme si tu cherchais la chose en tendant la main.

| ? Il y en a peut-être. | – Il n'y en a pas. |
|---|---|
| Tu cherches, tu te renseignes.<br>Is there any coffee? | Tu n'as rien trouvé.<br>There isn't any coffee. |

• **LE DÉTERMINANT "Ø" (ZÉRO)**
Nommer directement la boisson (*Ø milk*), l'aliment (*Ø meat*).
Tu colles seulement une étiquette. Tu ne précises pas la quantité.
Ø Water please! [L'important c'est que ce soit de l'eau, pas du vin !]

Pour offrir un jus de fruit à des invités, utilises-tu *"some"* ou *"any"* ? Justifie ton choix.

## *HAVE TO* + base verbale

Agir sans discuter, sans résister ! Ça ne se négocie même pas !

| + On n'a pas le choix ! |
|---|
| I / you, etc. have to go!<br>He / she has to go! |

| – On reste libre. | ? On se renseigne. |
|---|---|
| I / you, etc. don't have to go!<br>He / she doesn't have to go! | Do I / you, etc. have to go?<br>Does he / she have to go? |

*Have to* → prive de liberté, comme une "chaîne".
*Don't have to* → rend la liberté qu'on croyait perdue.

• **"HAD TO" + BASE VERBALE**
Dire ce qu'on a dû faire ou non, ce qu'il fallait faire ou non.
I had to get up at 6. I didn't have to tidy my tent. Did you have to?

## ENTRAÎNE-TOI

### Setting the scene

**1** ***Some, any* ou Ø ? Complète et réponds.**
1. Do you prefer ... tea or ... coffee?
2. Can I have ... more milk, please?
3. Are there ... sausages for breakfast?
4. There is ... ham, isn't there?
5. There weren't ... pears at the market.

### Scene 1

**2 Chez toi, quelles corvées te sont imposées ? Auxquelles échappes-tu ?**

**3 Invente des mini-dialogues.**
*Ex. :* You → *- What are you doing?*
*- I'm making my bed.*
*- Do you have to make your bed every day?*
1. Rob 2. the guides 3. Sophie

### Scene 2

**4 Pose la question pour obtenir le renseignement qui manque.**
1. The campers have to clean ...
2. They have to prepare ... every day.
3. Sophie has to ... once a day.
4. Yesterday, she had to iron ...
5. To get the Cook Badge, Aliette had to ...

**5 Comment dirais-tu que ... ?**
1. pour obtenir l'insigne de cuisinière, Aliette a dû préparer 15 repas.
2. elle n'a pas eu à faire les courses, mais elle a dû mettre le couvert.
3. il y avait beaucoup d'assiettes à laver.
4. heureusement, elle n'a pas été obligée d'aider sa mère ce jour-là!

Si tu proposes une boisson particulière, c'est qu'il y en a chez toi ! Tu diras donc *Do you want some fruit juice?*

# Grammar

MORE!
▶ EXERCISE BANK, P. 166
▶ GRAMMAR STORE, P. 142

## TROP OU PAS ASSEZ ?

**• TOO ...**

"Il y en a trop !" Ça dépasse la limite. Excessif.

too wet
adjectif

too much wind
nom sing.

too many clouds
nom plur.

**• NOT ENOUGH ...**

"Pas assez !" Le minimum n'est pas atteint.
La réalité est en-dessous de ce qu'on attendait.

not sunny enough — adjectif
not enough wind — nom sing.

⚠ Attention à l'ordre des mots.

Avec *sugar*, emploie-t-on *too much* ou *too many* ? Et avec *apples* ? *People* ?

| |
|---|
| too |
| MAXI |
| enough |
| MINI |
| not enough |

## COULD / COULDN'T

Possible ou non dans le passé.

She could sing when she was young. I couldn't open the door.

*Could* : "ça marchait". *Couldn't* : "ça coinçait".

## MUST / MUSTN'T, CAN / CAN'T

**• MUST / MUSTN'T:** contrôler ce qui se fait.

- *Must* : force qui pousse vers l'action = "pression pour".
I must write to Ben. You must go to bed! [bataille de volontés]
On veut vaincre une résistance.

- *Mustn't* : force qui éloigne de l'action = "pression contre".
He mustn't sell his car. You mustn't cry!
On veut empêcher que ça se fasse ou que ça continue.

**• CAN / CAN'T:** demander, accorder ou refuser une permission.
Can I go out? Yes, you can. / No, you can't.
*Can* : "pas de problème, ça passe". *Can't* : "ça bloque".

## SHOULD / SHOULDN'T

• **Conseiller, suggérer** : pousser sans forcer.
You should see a doctor. You should drive more slowly.

• **Reprocher, déconseiller**
You shouldn't eat too much chocolate.

⚠ *Can, could, must* et *should* sont des auxiliaires.
~~Do~~ et ~~to~~ sont donc interdits !

## ENTRAÎNE-TOI

### Scene 3

**6 Excessif ou insuffisant ? Complète puis termine les phrases.**

1. We had ... exercises to do, so I ...
2. There was ... traffic, so ...
3. Dad drives ... fast and Mum ...
4. These sausages are ... greasy! Don't ...
5. I put ... sugar in my tea, so I couldn't ...

**7 Réponds par la négative et explique.**

*Ex.* : Did Mark manage to open the jar?
→ *No, he couldn't open it. He wasn't strong enough / it was too hard.*

1. Did they manage to light the fire?
2. Did Aliette manage to take any photos?
3. Did she manage to make good batter?
4. Did they manage to eat the pancakes?
5. Did they manage to swim in the river?

### Scene 4

**8 Dessine le panneau.**

1. You often see this sign on country roads. You must look out for sheep.
2. When a driver sees this sign, he cannot go straight on. He has to turn left.
3. Drivers should always be very careful because children often cross here without looking left or right.
4. If you are riding your bike and you see this sign, get off or take another road.
5. This sign says you are on a special road and you can drive fast and safely.

**9 Quels conseils peux-tu formuler ?**

1. Mr Adams smokes 20 cigarettes a day.
2. An old lady is crossing the road.
3. Sophie's room is a real mess.
4. James's bicycle is making a funny noise.
5. Romeo is getting very fat.

**10 Qu'est-ce qui est permis, obligatoire ou interdit dans ces lieux ?**

1. in a plane or a train
2. in a zoo
3. in a church, a mosque, a synagogue

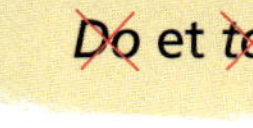

*Too much sugar* (substance, donc au singulier); *too many apples, people* (plusieurs unités, donc au pluriel).
*People* s'accorde toujours au pluriel : *Many people are waiting to see the doctor.*

workshop 3

# Do-it-yourself

## Make a compass!

YOU NEED:

- a bowl of water

- some washing-up liquid

- a cork

- a needle (about 3 cm)

- a magnet with north and south ends

- a knife

1 CUT A SLICE OF CORK ABOUT 1 CM THICK.

2 RUB THE POINT OF THE NEEDLE AGAINST THE NORTH END OF THE MAGNET.

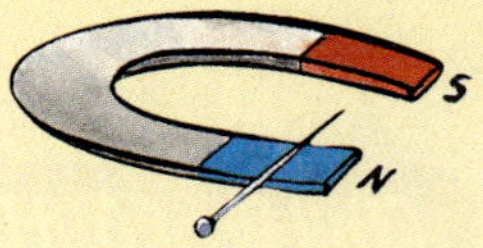


3 CAREFULLY PUSH THE NEEDLE THROUGH THE SLICE OF CORK.

4 PUT A TEASPOON OF WASHING-UP LIQUID INTO THE WATER.

5 PLACE THE CORK IN THE MIDDLE OF THE BOWL OF WATER. WATCH IT POINT NORTH!

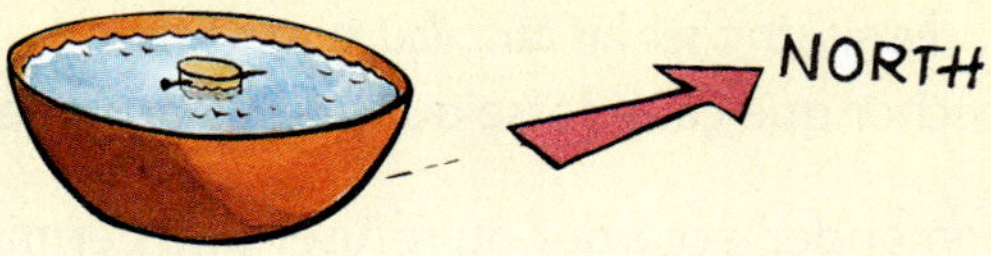


6 TELL THE CLASS WHAT HAPPENED.
I cut ..., I rubbed ..., I pushed ..., I put ... .

Find out about Scouts in America.
Prepare to tell the class.

# Project

## Quality medals!

YOU NEED: - scissors
- two cardboard circles
- coloured pens, pencils and ribbons.

- Make quality medals for two of your friends. Think of one special quality for each friend.
- On the front of each circle write the quality and draw a picture to represent it.
- On the back write one or two sentences to say why your friend should have this medal.

In class, compare the medals. Whose is best?

## Name scrabble game

1 Write the name of an English or American celebrity on a Bristol card. Be sure the name has 10 letters or more.

2 Put your cards together and turn over one card at a time. Who can write the most words using only the letters of the name?

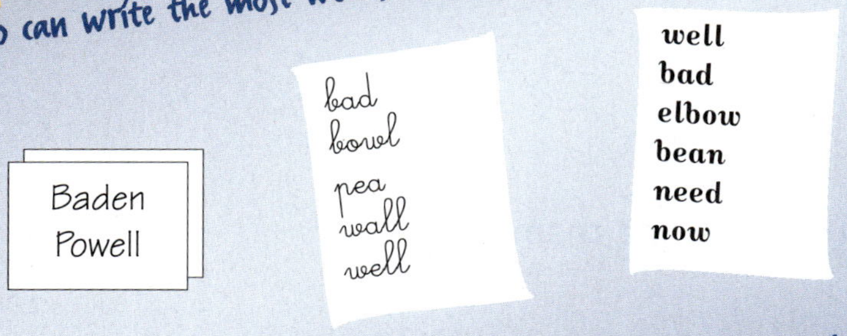


3 You can score 1 point for each correct word, and 5 for the longest word or for a word nobody else has got.

web site
www.spring.hachette-education.com

# ACT 4

## DANS CE CHAPITRE

### TU VAS T'EXERCER

- à parler de ta chambre.
- à dire quelles sont tes intentions et faire des suggestions.
- à parler de l'avenir : est-ce sûr, probable, peu probable ?
- à parler de ce que tu devras ou pourras faire.
- à lire pour découvrir quelques faits sur la Californie.

### TU VAS UTILISER

- *"will / may / might / shall".*
- *"will have to / will be able to".*
- *"if"* et *"when".*

### TU VAS REVOIR

- *"there is / there are".*
- *"have got".*
- *"be going to".*
- le vocabulaire pour décrire une chambre.

# Picture the future

# Setting the scene

▶ PARLE DE TA CHAMBRE.
▶ DIS CE QUE TU AS L'INTENTION DE FAIRE.

## At home

- A penny for your thoughts. Compare with your own room.

- Play and learn new words.
- Show you understand: what are the Macguires going to do?
- Your turn now!

**a. Talk about your plans after school today.**

Are you going to ...?

Yes, I am.

No, I'm not.

**b. Interview your teacher.**

A: What are you going to do tonight?
T: I am going to watch a video.
B: What are you going to see?
C: Who are you going to watch it with?

**HELP!**

**AFTER SCHOOL**
homework
meet friends
hobbies

shopping
chores

## forget-me-not

**Vérifie que tu sais...** - parler de tes intentions.
- décrire ta chambre.

He is going to watch a video, isn't he?
He isn't going to work, is he?

**"BE GOING TO" + V**
**The "go-future"**
*L'avenir, on s'y prépare !*

*On prévoit de ...*
I **am going to** watch a video.

*On s'attend à ...*
We **are going to** have fun.

*On devine la suite ...*
Look! It **is going to** rain.

**Rappelle-toi :** au moins cinq mots nouveaux pour parler de ta chambre.

# scene 1

▶ PARLE DE L'AVENIR : EST-CE SÛR ? PROBABLE ? PEU PROBABLE ?

## 1 SHOW YOU KNOW

- Say what you are going to do after the English lesson or after school today.
- Speak for 20 seconds non-stop about your room.

## 2 DISCOVER MORE

- Look and say what you can. Ask questions.

IAN AND JAMES:
TWO FRIENDS, TWO PETS, ONE DAY!
COME TO OUR FANCY DRESS BIRTHDAY PARTY ON JUNE 10TH.

Venue: on the Thames!

Time: boat will depart at 7pm from Westminster Pier and return at midnight.

And be prepared for an improvisation match!

RSVP

- Listen and find out more about the party.

## 3 YOUR TURN NOW!

- Say how old you will be on your next birthday. And in 2010, 2020, 2030?
- Find out whose birthdays are next month. Ask questions (plans, presents, etc.).

Are you going to have a party?
Yes, I am.
Will you invite ...?
Yes, I will / I may.
No, I won't.

- Magic lingo: Picture the future!

We're having a party on Saturday. It's going to be fun! Will you come?

## THINK AND STORE

**1** **Read and imagine the scene. Make sure you understand everything.**

**James** : Will you come to our birthday party next month, Mark?
**Mark** : I may, but I'm not sure. I might be in Paris that weekend.
**James** : We're having an improvisation match! You really must come.
**Mark** : I'll do my best. What are you going to wear?
**James** : I won't tell you. It's a secret. But Rob is going to be a Maharajah and Aliette is going to be Joan of Arc.
**Mark** : If I come, I'll dress up as an Egyptian mummy!
**James** : That's a brilliant idea!
**Mark** : How many people will there be?
**James** : 35. And I've invited Ben, Julie and Sharon. But they won't come.
**Mark** : They might! Who knows? By the way, how old will you be?
**James** : We'll both be 14 and Romeo and Juliet will be 4. We were all born on the same day.
**Mark** : Are the dogs going to dress up too?

**HELP!**

improvi**sa**tion

**se**cret

to dress up as: to wear a disguise

by the way: *à propos*

**2** **Lines 1-5: pick out the different verb forms which refer to the future.**

**3** **Open your workbook and learn your lesson step by step.**

▶ EXERCISES AND GRAMMAR: PAGE 96.

## forget-me-not

**Vérifie que tu sais...** - parler de l'avenir : est-ce certain, probable, peu probable ?

Mark may not go to James's party, but Sophie will.

*Imaginer l'avenir*
*Pré-voir, pré-dire*

**"WILL"**
*Donne une image claire.*
*Sûr et certain !*
He will come.
≠
He will not come.

He'll

He won't

**"MAY"**
*Dessine en pointillés.*
*Pas très sûr !*
He may (not) come.

**"MIGHT"**
*C'est juste esquissé.*
*Pas sûr du tout !*
He might (not) come.

**Rappelle-toi :** comment indiquer ton âge.
- *Au passé :* I was 12 last year.
- *Au présent :* I am 13 now.
- *Au futur :* I will be 14 next month.

# scene 2

▶ DIS CE QUE TU FERAS,
À QUELLE CONDITION ET QUAND.

## 1 SHOW YOU KNOW

- Talk about Ian and James's birthday party.
- Ask your teacher about her / his next dinner party.

## 2 SPRING INTO ACTION

- Look and talk about the cards. Match them with the greetings.
- Listen and choose the card.

a. To Peter, hoping you will have a lovely birthday!

b. ... to stay in bed! Hope you will be back on your feet real soon!

c. ... So I won't go out from now on.

d. OF COURSE I WILL!

e. ... from the one who looked for it, paid for it and posted it (and from the other one!).

f. A star is born!

g. Good luck and keep working!

h. I WILL ALWAYS LOVE YOU!

- **Listen: If! If! If!**
- **On the board, start sentences like this with your teacher.**

| IF | WHEN |
|---|---|
| If it rains tomorrow ...<br>If ... next week ... | When I am 18 ...<br>When I get home tonight ... |

- **Now say what you will / won't do if and when ...**
  A: If it rains tomorrow, I'll go to the cinema. I won't ... .
- **Write five promises: to your parents, to your teacher, to friends.**

▶ PLAY AND LEARN IN YOUR WORKBOOK.
▶ EXERCISES AND GRAMMAR: PAGE 96.

## SAY IT!

**Chris**~~t~~mas

aɪ
**Va**lentine

anni**vers**~~a~~ry

ʌ
husband

ʌ
son

uː
soon

kjuːt
cute

## forget-me-not

**Vérifie que tu sais...** - te projeter dans l'avenir avec *"if"* et *"when"*.
- t'engager à faire quelque chose.

She will marry him if and when he cuts his hair.

**"WHEN"**

*On s'installe dans la réalité future.*
When I **am** 18, I **will** ...

**"IF"**

*On simule une réalité.*
If you cut your hair, I will ...

*Avec* **will**, *on garantit, on s'engage à ...*

**Rappelle-toi :** à quelle occasion on envoie des cartes.
- for a birthday, an anniversary, Valentine's Day, Christmas and New Year.
- when people move house, pass a test, are ill, get married, have a new baby.

# scene 3

▶ FAIS DES SUGGESTIONS.
▶ DONNE TON AVIS.

## 1 SHOW YOU KNOW

- Listen and play the "If game" with Mark.

## 2 DISCOVER MORE

- Look and say what you can. What will they do if they go there?

**CLASS TRIP**

**Transport by school bus:**
**departure 6am June 8th - return 9pm June 10th**

**Choose your destination! Sign up before next Monday!**

cost $50 (hotel)

$40 (youth hostel)
Jaws, Star Wars, Jurassic Park

$30 (tent campsite)
rafting, surfing, riding, biking, wildlife viewing

**In charge:** Mr and Mrs Rodriguez

- Listen: where do they choose to go? What will they do there?

## 3 YOUR TURN NOW!

- Suggest a class trip. Choose places of interest in your region.

"Shall we go to ...?" "No, let's go to ... instead."

- Vote for the final decision. Suggest what to take and do.
- Magic Lingo: The art of persuasion.

**HELP!**

**Suggestions**
Shall we ...?
Let's ... .
What about ...ing?

**Reactions**
+
Good idea!
Yes, let's!
Why not!
I'd like to!
–
No, let's ... instead.

"Where shall we go?" "Let's go to the movies, let's go and see the stars!"

## THINK AND STORE

**1** **Read and imagine the scene. Make sure you understand everything.**

**Alec** : Shall we sign up for the trip next month? I'd like to go to Disneyland.
**Sue** : No, let's go to Universal Studios instead.
**Alec** : Again! We went there three years ago.
**Sue** : And we went to Disneyland four years ago.
**Alec** : So let's go to Redwood National Park, shall we? We'll go hiking and have a camp fire in the evening.
**Sue** : And we'll see bears, and the world's tallest trees!
**All** : Yes! Why not? Good idea! Let's do that!

**Sue** : OK. I'll call Ben.
Ben, It's Sue. What about going to Redwood National Park for our class trip?
**Ben** : Good idea! But I won't be here. *(Sneezes)*
**Sue** : You won't? Where will you be?
**Ben** : In London. *(Sneezes)*
**Sue** : London, Ohio?
**Ben** : No, London, England of course!

### HELP!

e
ins**tead**: in place of

aɪ
hiking: walking

eə
a bear

aɪ
id**e**a

**2** **Count all the expressions used to make suggestions.**

**3** **Open your workbook and learn your lesson step by step.**

▶ **EXERCISES AND GRAMMAR: PAGE 97.**

## forget-me-not

**Vérifie que tu sais...** - faire des suggestions.
- consulter les autres et donner ton avis.

He wants to go to Disneyland but she doesn't.

*Ton avis m'intéresse !*

**"SHALL WE?"**
*Décider ensemble.*
Shall we visit the studios?

**"LET'S ..., SHALL WE?"**
*Entraîner les autres.*
Let's go now, shall we?

**Rappelle-toi :** cinq activités possibles dans un parc national.

# scene 4

▶ PARLE DE CE QU'IL FAUDRA FAIRE, DE CE QU'IL SERA POSSIBLE DE FAIRE.

## 1 SHOW YOU KNOW

- Suggest a weekend activity to a friend. (S)He reacts.

## 2 SPRING INTO ACTION

- Look and say what you can about the shed. Ask questions.
- Listen and learn how to talk about future obligations.

- Listen: plans for the shed. Who will do what?

**HELP!**

**DIY (Do-it-yourself)**
- re**pair** (GB) / fix (US)
- re**place** / change
- in**stall** the elec**tri**city
- paint / decorate the walls
- make cushions
- clean, etc.

- **When the den is finished, what will be different for Ben?**

## SAY IT!

listen to

aɪ
organize

aɪ
in**vite**

aɪ
spider

▶ PLAY AND LEARN IN YOUR WORKBOOK.
▶ EXERCISES AND GRAMMAR: PAGE 97.

## forget-me-not

WB

**Vérifie que tu sais...** - parler de ce qu'il faudra faire.
- dire ce qu'il sera possible de faire.

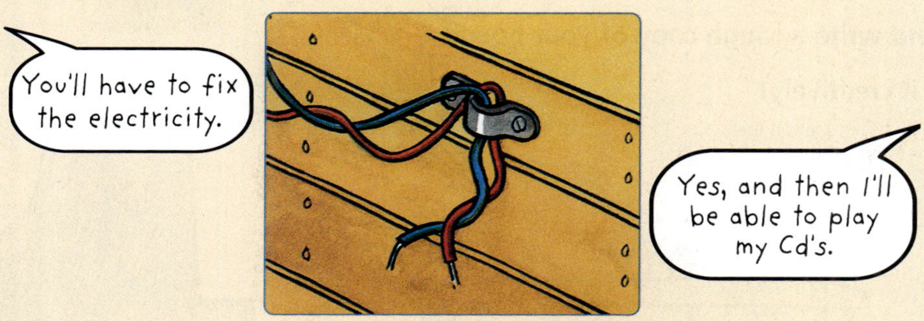


First they will have to fix the electricity.
Then Ben will be able to listen to his Cd's.

*S'engager sur l'avenir*

**"WILL"**

*On se porte volontaire.*
I will help you.
*On garantit que ça se fera.*
Uncle J. will fix the roof.

**"WILL BE ABLE TO"**

*Ça, on pourra le faire !*
I **will be able to** help you.

**"WILL HAVE TO"**

*Ça, il faudra le faire !*
You **will have to** fix it.

**Rappelle-toi :** ce qu'il faut faire pour rénover une pièce.

# Put pen to paper

## 1 Read two poems.

a. A.A. Milne wrote "Winnie the Pooh" and poems for his son, Christopher. Read this one. What was Christopher's favourite place?

b. Chloé is a French pupil. What about her favourite place?

Halfway down the stairs
Is a stair
Where I sit.

There isn't any
Other stair
Quite like it.

I'm not at the bottom;
I'm not at the top.

So this is the stair
Where
I always
Stop. [...]

A.A. Milne, 1924.

## 2 Write it yourself!

a. Write a poem about a place you like.

**POEM**
What is your favourite place? Is it a secret?
Describe it. How do you feel there?

Need help? Workbook!

b. Collect your ideas and write a rough copy of your poem.

c. Copy it out. Present it creatively!

# scene 5

**DÉCOUVRE LA CALIFORNIE.**
- ▶ Dis ce que tu sais.
- ▶ Prépare-toi.
- ▶ Lis.

# Earthquakes in California

## 1 WHAT DO YOU KNOW?

- Say what you can about California.

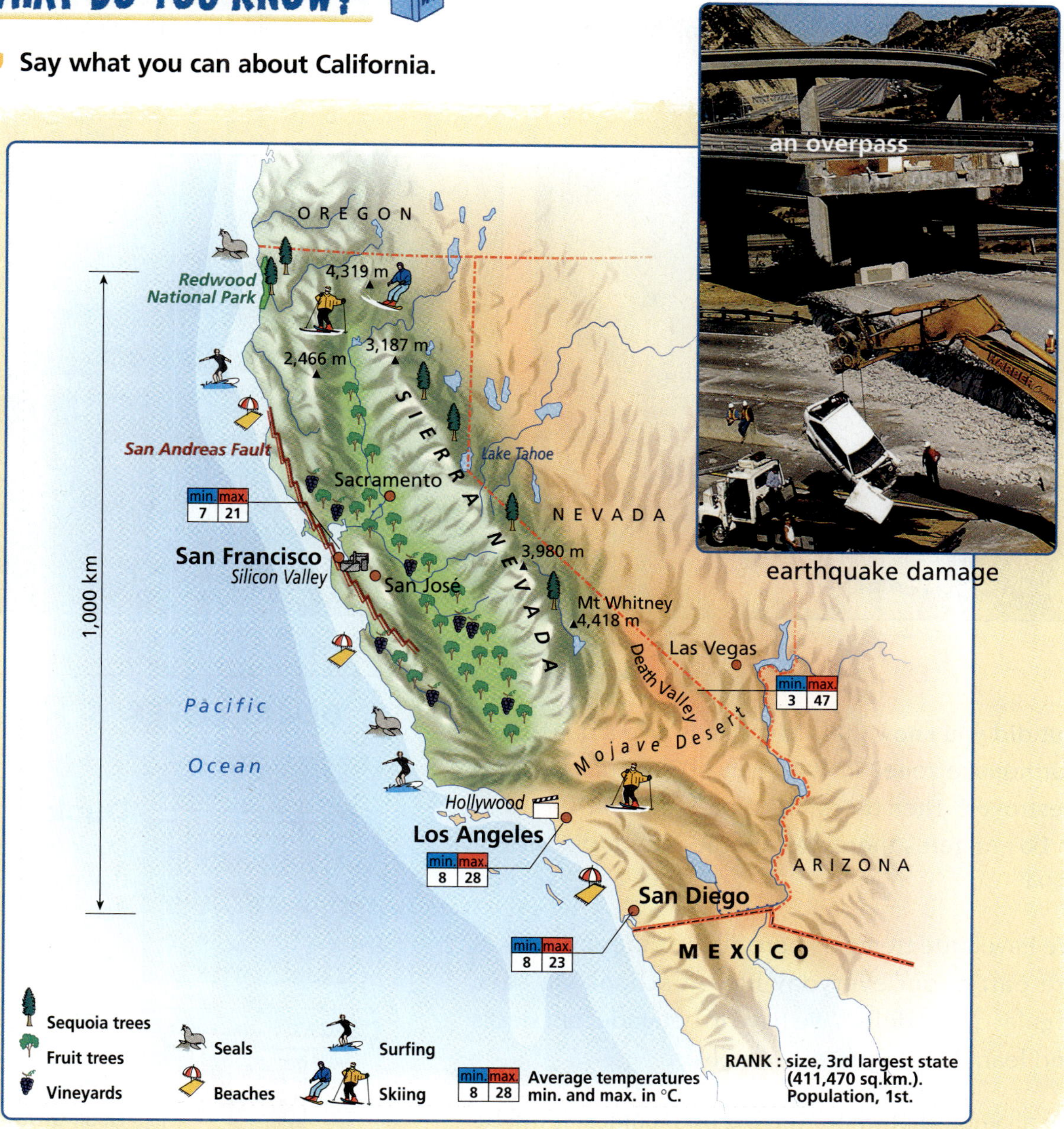

earthquake damage

## 2 PREPARE TO READ

- You are going to read about earthquakes in California. These words are in the text. Match them by opposites: dangerous ≠ safe.

danger — an underpass — outside — to panic — inside — to destroy — safety — to die
to build — an overpass — to survive — to crouch — to stay calm — to stand

# scene 5

## 3 SPRING INTO ENGLISH

- **Reading strategies: use the context to understand the words marked *.**

I was born in San Francisco, which I adore. Living in California is great. We have everything here: warm sun, the ocean, the mountains, the desert, even film stars and Disneyland!

1

2

But did you know that California is also a dangerous earthquake zone? In 1906, 80% of San Francisco was destroyed. Then there was a big quake in 1989 and in Los Angeles there was another major disaster in 1994.

We have little tremors* here all the time and quakes are part of our everyday life. At school, we have regular quake drills*. We have to get under our desks and learn how to protect ourselves.

We all know that when "the big one" comes, it will be very serious. Where will I be when it happens? Will people panic? Will the house resist the quake? How much damage will there be? If we are in the car, will we be able to find a safe place to stop? Will I be injured*, or even die?

Well, there's no point worrying, is there?
After all: "What will be will be! The future's not ours to see!"

### DUCK, COVER & HOLD!

**Duck**
Duck or drop down on the floor.

**Cover**
Take COVER under a sturdy* desk or table, or protect your head and neck with your arms.

**Hold**
If you take cover under a sturdy piece of furniture, HOLD on to it and be prepared to move with it.

# 10 things to help you survive during an earthquake

**Californians are constantly aware of the potential of an earthquake creating damage and creating dangerous conditions. So if we don't properly prepare, the next quake may cause greater personal damage than necessary. Each item listed below won't stop the next earthquake but it may help you survive in a better way.**

## 4 basics to do during an earthquake

1. STAY CALM.
2. Inside: Stand in a doorway, or crouch under a desk or table, away from windows or glass dividers.
3. Outside: Stand away from buildings, trees, telephone and electric lines.
4. On the road: Drive away from underpasses / overpasses; stop in a safe area; stay in vehicle.

## 6 basics to do after an earthquake

1. Check for injuries. Provide first aid.
2. Check for safety. Check for gas, water, sewage breaks[1]; check for downed electric lines and shorts; turn off appropriate utilities; check for building damage and potential safety problems during aftershocks such as cracks around chimney and foundation.
3. Clean up dangerous spills[2].
4. Wear shoes.
5. Turn on radio and listen for instructions from public safety agencies.
6. Don't use the telephone except for emergency use.

American Red Cross

Prepare! for the QUAKE

1 breaks (*ici*) : *ruptures de canalisations*
2 spills (*ici*) : *écoulements*

## 4 LISTEN

- Check! Right or wrong?
- Listen for more: Earthquake emergency supplies.

www.redcross.org

# Encore

## 1 REACT

## 2 READ

- **Read and show you understand.**

**THE INTERNET CHARTER**

1. I will only give my e-mail address to people I know.
2. I will respect my school's or parents' rules for using the web.
3. I will not spend too much time connected.
4. I will always make sure the modem is disconnected when I have finished.
5. I will never meet anyone I have corresponded with on the web without permission.
6. I will not put my photograph on a web site.
7. I will not buy anything on the web without permission.
8. I will tell an adult if I discover anything which worries or upsets me.

## 3 LISTEN

- **Oral comprehension.**
  Promises, promises!

- **Phonetics and dictation.**
  Ben in London.

# Oral recap.

- **Say the words aloud!**

**Name five things near your bed!**

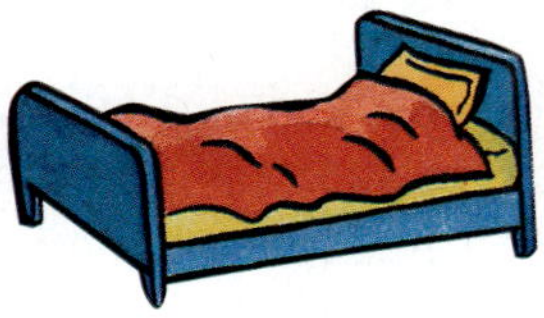

**Name five things in your bathroom!**

**Name five actions decorators do!**

- **Say the words and then spell aloud!**

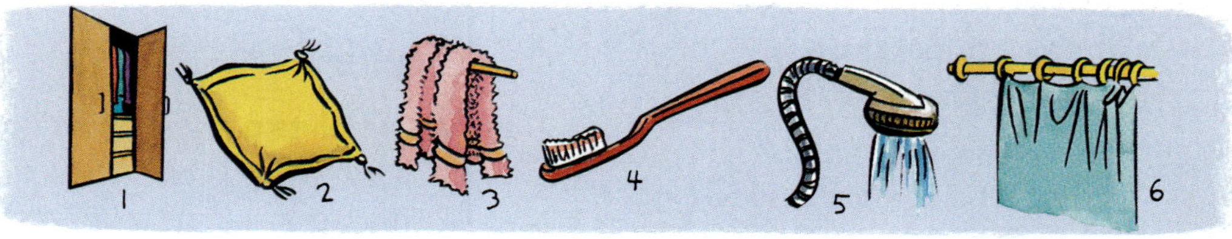


- **Find the odd one out and then make a series for the class.**

cloudy - windy - sunny - rainy - funny - snowy
repair - change - decorate - congratulate - clean - wash - paint
birthday card - anniversary card - Valentine's card - Christmas card - New Year's card - identity card

- **Talk about your intentions.**

This afternoon I am going to ...
but I am not going to ...

# Word builder

- **Make as many compound words as you can.**

bed day bath birth
school radio tooth arm
bag hair book alarm
room clock brush chair

a clock radio

- **Choose two of the words and give the definition.**

A clock radio is a radio with a clock inside / that has a clock inside.

Compound nouns: the *last noun* gives the *category*.
A bedside table is a table.

# Grammar

L'avenir, c'est demain, mais ça s'imagine maintenant. Voilà pourquoi l'anglais utilise le présent en *be + -ing* et des expressions comme *be going to ...*, *will ...*, etc. qui sont techniquement au présent.

En français, utilise-t-on parfois le présent pour parler de l'avenir ?

## *BE GOING TO* + base verbale

- On appelle *be going to* *"the go-future"*. On se dirige déjà *(going)* vers l'action *(to)* : "c'est bien parti pour se faire !"

On prévoit de ... I'm going to have a party.
On prédit que ... Look! It is going to rain.

- Le présent conduit "naturellement" au futur.

– cassette louée → I'm going to watch a video [= suite normale]
– histoire très triste → They are going to cry [= suite logique]

Le *to* de *be going to* fait penser au *to* de *to London, to school*, etc., mais cette fois-ci la "destination", c'est une action :

She's going to sing.

## *WILL / MAY / MIGHT* + base verbale

On prend position sur l'avenir.

- **WILL** : "Sûr que ça se fera !" Pas d'obstacle. Réalisation garantie.

– On s'engage à faire l'action (comme un contrat qu'on signe).
I'll dress up as an Egyptian. ["c'est entendu", "compte dessus"]
– On connaît la réalité future (image claire et nette dans la tête)
James will be 14 next month. [je le sais : c'est sûr !]
– On se porte volontaire ou on décide sur le champ.
I'll call Ben. I'll help you prepare the party.

- **WON'T** : "Ça ne se fera pas : c'est sûr !"

– On ne veut pas faire l'action qui est demandée, espérée.
I won't tell you. It's a secret.
– On sait très bien que ça ne se fera pas.
Ben won't come.

- **MAY / MAY NOT** : "Pas très sûr, ça se fera peut-être."

I may (not) have a party.

- **MIGHT / MIGHT NOT** : "Qui peut le dire ?" "Impossible de savoir !"

Mark might (not) be in Paris that weekend.

*May* et *might* contiennent deux images :
– celle d'un obstacle qui peut surgir et gêner l'action.
– celle d'une bifurcation qui peut mener vers une autre action.
Voilà pourquoi on n'est jamais complètement sûr que ça se fera !

⚠ *Will, may* et *might* sont des modaux. ~~Do~~ et ~~to~~ interdits !

## ENTRAÎNE-TOI

### Setting the scene

**1 Imagine ce qui va se passer.**

1. Sophie is switching on her computer.
2. Her father is measuring her room.
3. She is going into the bathroom.
4. Now she is opening her cupboard.
5. She is picking up her paint brush.

### Scene 1

**2 Complète par *will / won't* ou *may*.**

1. Aliette's Dad ... be 50 on June 25th.
2. The weather ... be cold, will it?
3. He ... not have a party. He isn't sure.
4. The stars say he ... live a long life.
5. Aliette hasn't decided, but she ... buy him a DVD.

**3 Réponds par *will, may* ou *might*, puis donne une explication.**

*Ex. :* Will you go out tonight?
→ *No, I won't. I have too much work.*

1. Will you have a shower tonight?
2. Will you be in 4e next year?
3. Where will you be next July?
4. Will you dress up for your birthday?
5. What will you buy next time you go shopping for clothes?

### Scene 2

**4 Mets le verbe à la forme qui convient. (voir *if* et *when*, p. 97)**

1. He (have) a party if he (pass) his exam.
2. She (not go) to school if she (be) ill.
3. If you (cut) your hair, I (be) pleased.
4. When he (be) 16, he (learn) to drive.
5. I (be) happy when Mum (buy) a new rug.

**5 Termine les phrases.**

1. The scouts won't light the fire if ...
2. If Rob isn't careful on his bike, ...
3. Mark will stop acting when ...
4. When I am on holiday, ...
5. When I am 20, ...

Oui, pour parler de déplacements, de choses programmées : „j'arrive demain à 8h", „on déménage en septembre".

# Grammar

MORE!
▶ EXERCISE BANK, P. 168
▶ GRAMMAR STORE, P. 142

## IF & WHEN

Ouvrir, créer, visiter "l'espace futur".

• **IF** + verbe au présent : ce n'est pas gagné !
On simule une situation future, on pose une condition.

*If you cut your hair, I'll marry you!*

Ça se fera si la condition *(if ...)* est remplie.

• **WHEN** + verbe au présent : c'est gagné d'avance !
J'anticipe sur le futur. C'est aussi sûr que si c'était maintenant !

*When I am 18, I'll learn to drive a car.*

Traduis la dernière phrase. Quels temps emploie-t-on en français?

## SUGGÉRER ET PROPOSER

• **SHALL WE / SHALL I ...?**
Suggérer une activité et inviter les autres à donner leur avis :

*Shall we watch a video? Shall I open the window?*

• **LET'S ...**
– Entraîner les autres vers une activité.

*Let's have a party. Let's invite all our friends.*

– *Shall we?* peut être ajouté en *tag*.

*Let's have a party, shall we?*

– *Let's* est la contraction de *let us* (pronom personnel complément correspondant à *we*.) *Let's* est toujours suivi de la base verbale.

## WILL / WON'T HAVE TO

Pourra-t-on échapper à l'action, oui ou non ?

| + |
|---|
| On n'y échappera pas ! I will have to help, etc. |

| ? | – |
|---|---|
| Pourra-t-on y échapper ? Will I have to help? Etc. | On pourra y échapper ! I won't have to help, etc. |

## WILL / WON'T BE ABLE TO

Sera-t-on en mesure de faire l'action, ou non ?

| + |
|---|
| Ce sera possible. Conditions favorables ! I will be able to help, etc. |

| ? | – |
|---|---|
| Possible ? Will I be able to help? Etc. | Impossible ! I won't be able to help, etc. |

## ENTRAÎNE-TOI

### Scene 3

**6 Compose trois mini-dialogues :**
**"A" suggère une activité.**
**"B" refuse et en propose une autre.**
**"C" accepte avec / sans enthousiasme.**

**7 Refuse et explique-toi.**
1. Let's go for a hike, shall we?
2. Why not go roller-blading?
3. Shall we visit the British Museum?
4. What about going to the shops?
5. Will you help me tidy my room?

### Scene 4

**8 Complète par *will / won't have to* ou *will / won't be able to*.**
1. Ben ... change the window himself.
2. Uncle Jim ... repair it. He is very clever.
3. Mrs Adams is sorry but she ... help.
4. She ... work in the shed. She's ill.
5. She ... stay in bed for 10 days.

**9 *Will / won't? May / might? Shall?***
1.... I make the cushions or buy them?
2. I know Ben ... be very happy in his shed.
3. He ... be there now. Go and see.
4. When it is finished, he ... invite his friends.
5. Alec is sorry he ... be able to come.

**10 Complète et réponds.**
1. How old ... you be in 2035?
2. When ... you be 45?
3. Where ... Mark going next June?
4. What second language ... you ... study next year?
5. ... you ... study Japanese?

En français, on emploie le futur dans les deux propositions : Quand / lorsque j'**aurai** 18 ans, je **conduirai**. En anglais, on emploie le présent dans la subordonnée avec *when*.

# Do-it-yourself

## Make a prediction wheel!

YOU NEED:
- three cardboard circles (radius: 65 mm, 85 mm, 105 mm)
- a pencil and some coloured pens
- a split pin

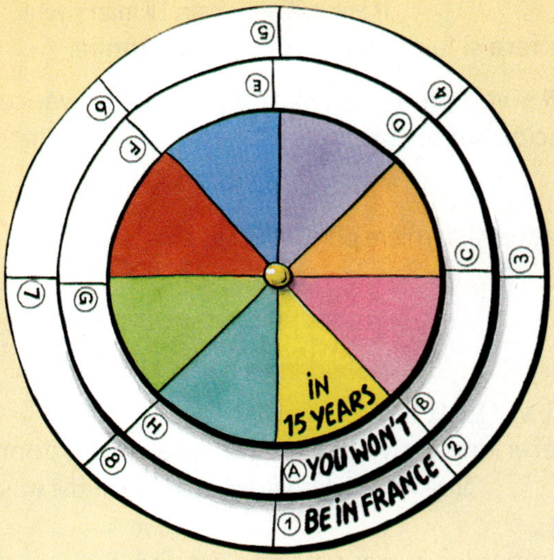


1 SEPARATE EACH CIRCLE INTO 8 SECTIONS AND ATTACH THE THREE CIRCLES WITH THE SPLIT PIN.

2 SMALL CIRCLE: COLOUR EACH SECTION A DIFFERENT COLOUR AND THEN WRITE A TIME IN THE FUTURE: NEXT SUMMER, TOMORROW, IN 15 YEARS, ETC.

3 MIDDLE CIRCLE: IN EACH SECTION WRITE A LETTER A, B, C, ETC., AND THE BEGINNING OF A PREDICTION: YOU WILL / WON'T / MAY / MIGHT. REPEAT TWICE.

4 LARGE CIRCLE: IN EACH SECTION WRITE A NUMBER AND THE REST OF THE PREDICTIONS: LIVE IN ... / GET MARRIED / FIND A ... / HAVE ..., ETC.

5 IN PAIRS: ASK A FRIEND TO CHOOSE A COLOUR, A LETTER FROM A TO H AND A NUMBER FROM 1 TO 8. THEN CONNECT THE COLOUR, THE LETTER AND THE NUMBER AND READ THE PREDICTION.

OK! Red ... A ... 1.

In 15 years you won't ...!

**Find 3 pieces of information about an American National Park.**

# Project

## My dream house

Think of your dream house!

- It can be on the water, in a tree, under the ground, in France, abroad, in space!
- It can be any size: from a one-room house to a palace!
- It can have all the comforts you wish!
- Say what you will be able to do in this house.
- Make a collage using photos and drawings. Draw the floor plan if you want.

## Guess my future job game

1 Choose a job you might like to do.

2 Write 3 things you will / won't have to do: "If I am a ... I will have to read a lot of names."

3 Read ONE sentence to a friend and he will try to guess your job.

"I will have to wear a uniform."

"Do you want to be a policeman?"

4 Continue reading one sentence at a time until he guesses right.

5 Now guess another person's future job!

Vote for the best dream house in the class!

web site @ www.spring.hachette-education.com

# ACT 5

## DANS CE CHAPITRE

### TU VAS T'EXERCER

- à décrire le physique d'une personne.
- à parler de ressemblances et de différences.
- à parler de records.
- à dire ce que tu as déjà fait ou non.
- à lire un extrait de magazine pour jeunes.

### TU VAS UTILISER

- le comparatif.
- le superlatif.
- le *present perfect.*

### TU VAS REVOIR

- le prétérit.
- *"ago".*

# Me and my world

# Setting the scene

▶ DÉCRIS QUELQU'UN.
▶ PARLE DE RESSEMBLANCES ET COMPARE.

## Looks

- A penny for your thoughts! Say what you can and ask questions.

1

2

4

3

- Play and learn: discover new words.
- Who do they look like? What do they have in common?
- Your turn now!

a. Say who you look like and compare.

I look like my cousin. I've got the same eyes but my hair is longer.

I look like my brother but I am not as athletic.

b. Say what you'd like to have in common with your favourite star.

A: I'd like to have ...'s eyes / hair.

**HELP!**

**...er than**
small ≠ tall
thin > slim > plump > fat
fit, strong
healthy, sporty

**more ... than**
athletic
attractive
charming

**better ... than**
well-dressed

5

6

7

8

## forget-me-not

**Vérifie que tu sais...** - te décrire et décrire une autre personne.
- parler de ressemblances et comparer.

Who does Michael look like?

He looks like his father.

Michael Douglas looks like his father, doesn't he?
They have got the same dimple, haven't they?

### COMPARER C'EST JUGER

***Pareil !***
I am **as tall as** you (are).

***Pas pareil !***
I am **not as tall as** you (are).

***Plus !***
*Adjectifs courts*
I am tall**er than** you (are).
*Adjectifs longs*
I'm **more** athletic **than** you (are).

**Rappelle-toi :** au moins cinq mots nouveaux pour décrire une personne.

# scene 1

▶ PARLE DE RECORDS DANS TA FAMILLE ET DANS LA CLASSE.

## 1 SHOW YOU KNOW

- Describe someone in the class. Your friends must guess who it is.
- Compare a friend to someone in her / his family.

## 2 DISCOVER MORE

- Look and say what you can.

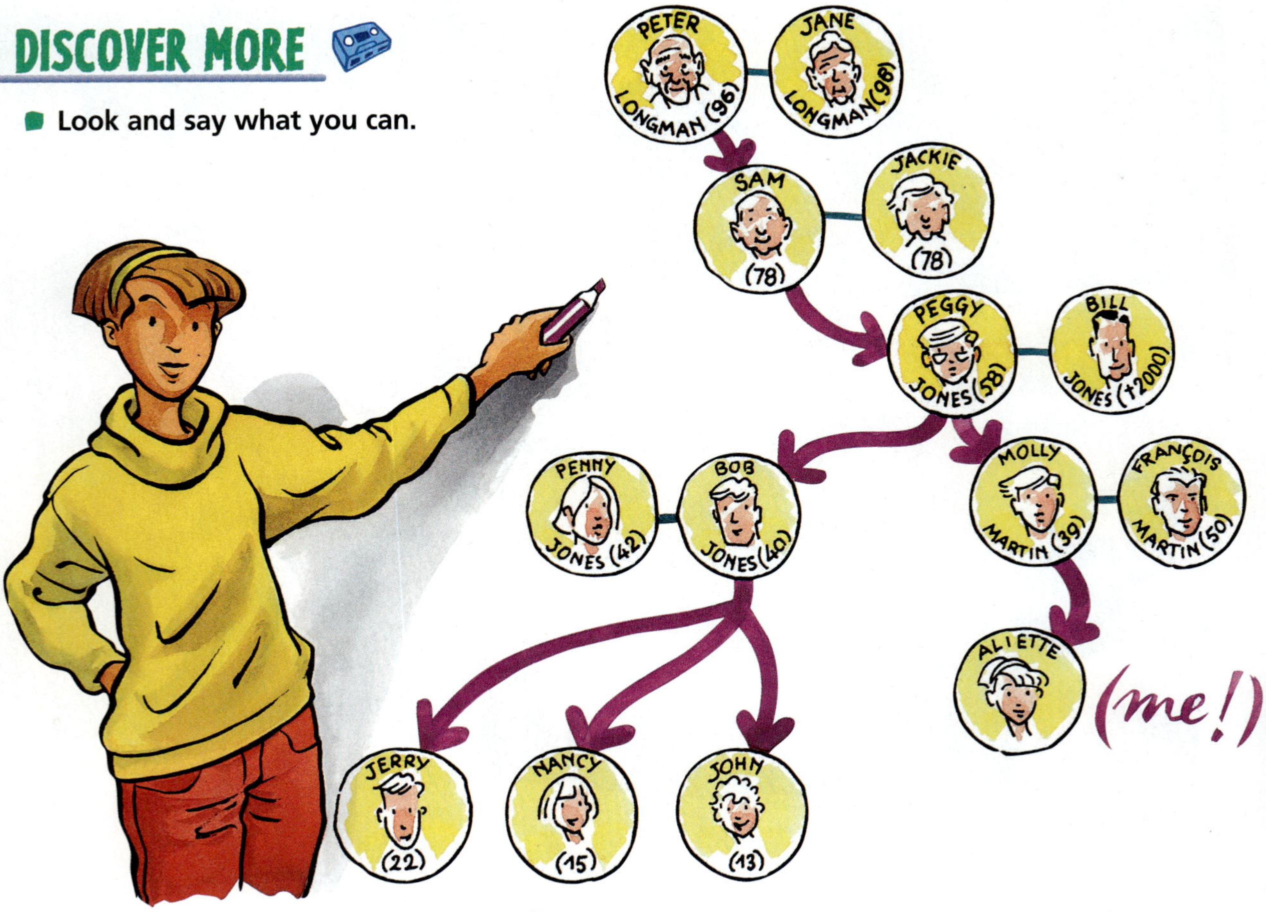


- Listen: the Challenger's Game. What are their records?

## 3 YOUR TURN NOW!

- Records in your families. Ask questions.

> My grandfather is the oldest person in my family. Who is the oldest in yours?

- Records in the class: listen and follow our instructions.
- Magic Lingo: Go for the best!

**HELP!**

**The ...est**

young ≠ old — small ≠ tall
slim ≠ fat — tidy ≠ messy
pretty - smart - strong - lazy

**The most ...**

musical - ar**tis**tic - ath**le**tic
**amu**sing - patient
hardworking, ...

**The best / the worst at ...**

drawing - cooking - singing, ...

*The best music, the finest lyrics, the most fabulous voices! It's top of the pops!*

## THINK AND STORE

**1** **Read and imagine the scene. Make sure you understand everything.**

*It is Aliette's great great-grandparents' diamond wedding anniversary. Mark is organizing a challenge game.*

**Jane** : I think I am the oldest person here. Any challengers?
**Mark** : That was easy, Mrs Longman! Mr Longman?
**Peter** : Well, I have the longest hands, I think. They're 23 cm long!
**Jerry** : I challenge you! Mine are longer! Look!
**Peter** : You're right, Jerry. It runs in the family! Who's next?
**Together** : Uncle Bob! Uncle Bob!
**Bob** : A record? Well, I'm probably the best pianist here!
**Aliette** : I challenge you, Uncle Bob!
**Mark** : So let's see! Aliette, you start! *(piano)*

**Bob** : I'm out! My niece definitely plays better! Molly, you're next.
**Molly** : I'm sure I'm the most talkative! I can talk on the phone for six hours non-stop! Any challengers? No? François, your turn.
**François** : I think I am the fastest at *"calcul mental"*, er, adding.
**John** : I challenge you, Uncle! Give us a sum to do, Mark.
**Mark** : Who is the fastest? Uncle or nephew? Ready? Steady? Go!
**John** : 17,678,934! *(applause)*

**2** **Pick out all the superlatives. How many have you got?**

**3** **Open your workbook and learn your lesson step by step.**

▶ EXERCISES AND GRAMMAR: PAGE 118.

### HELP!

**re**cord

**chal**lenge

hand

It runs in the family: it is a characteristic.

good
better
the best

**tal**kative (l barré)

**ne**phew (ph = f)

2 + 2 = a sum: you add two and two

## forget-me-not

**Vérifie que tu sais...** - parler de records.

Aliette's great great-grandmother is the oldest in her family.

**Rappelle-toi :** ces rapports de parenté.
- (great) grandfather and grandmother - husband and wife
- son and daughter - uncle and aunt [ɑːnt] - nephew and niece [niːs]

### LE SUPERLATIF
***Le plus !***

*Adjectifs "courts"*
**the** old**est** ...
**the** clever**est** ...
**the** mess**iest** ...

*Adjectifs longs*
**the most** talkative

⚠
**good** → better → **the best**
**bad** → worse → **the worst**

# scene 2

▶ DÉCOUVRE DES RECORDS.
▶ PARLE DE DIMENSIONS ET DE MESURES.

## 1 SHOW YOU KNOW

- **Ask your teacher questions about records in her / his family.**

## 2 SPRING INTO ACTION

- **Records in America. Look and say what you can. Ask questions.**
  A: I suppose the Sears Tower is the ... skyscraper in the USA. How high is it?
- **Listen for more information.**

1. The Verazzano Bridge, New York

2. The Mississippi River

3. The San Diego Zoo, California

4. The Sears Tower, Chicago

- **Now talk about these records. Compare with France.**
  A: Rhode Island is the smallest state. It is ... .

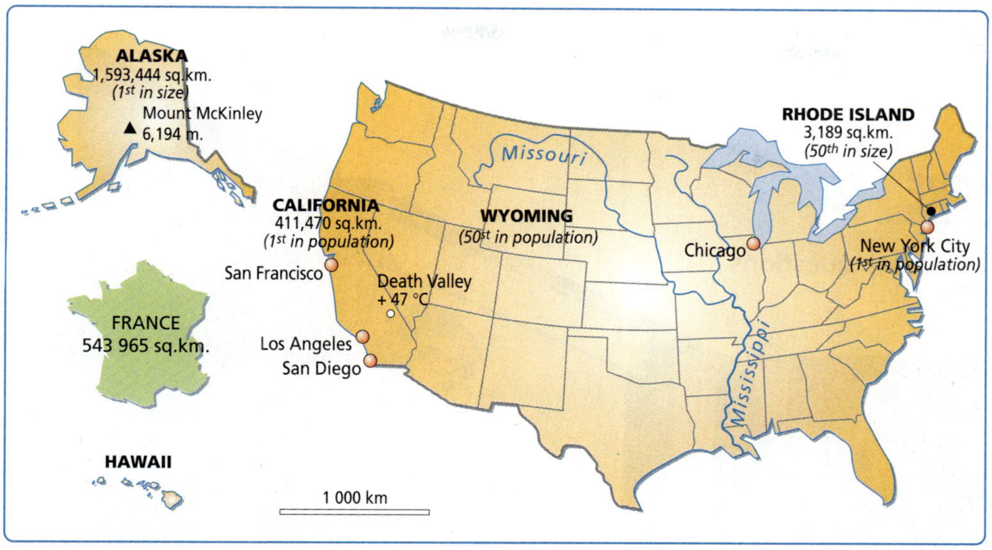


- **Listen: the geography quiz. How many questions can you answer?**
- **In pairs, write questions using a superlative (geography, history, zoology, etc.). Read them out and select the five best. Look up the answers for next time.**

*Which animal runs the fastest?*

*Who was the youngest / the oldest American president?*

▶ PLAY AND LEARN IN YOUR WORKBOOK.
▶ EXERCISES AND GRAMMAR: PAGE 118.

## SAY IT!

əʊ
Rhode I~~s~~land

ə
Alaska

aʊ
Mount

sɪəz taʊə
the Sears Tower

the Missis**sip**pi river

ɑː
the Verazzano bridge

popu**la**tion

## forget-me-not

**Vérifie que tu sais...** - parler de records, de dimensions et de mesures.

How high is it?

It is 6,194 metres high.

Mount McKinley is the highest mountain in the United States, isn't it?

### "HOW" + ADJ.

*âge*
**How old** is it?

*dimension*
**How big** is it?

*hauteur*
**How tall** is it?
**How high** is it?

*longueur*
**How long** is it?

**Rappelle-toi :** comment dire les grands nombres.

1,000 one thousand   10,000 ten thousand   100,000 a hundred thousand   1,000,000 one million

⚠ 145,789 one hundred **and** forty five thousand, seven hundred **and** eighty nine.

# scene 3

▶ PARLE DE VOYAGES.
▶ DIS OÙ TU ES DÉJÀ ALLÉ(E).

## 1 SHOW YOU KNOW

- **Talk about records in the USA, in France and in the world.**

## 2 DISCOVER MORE

- **Say what you can. Ask questions.**

- **Listen: Mark's experiences. What countries has he been to?**

## 3 YOUR TURN NOW!

- **Ask your friend and then your teacher where they have been. Write the names of the places on the board.**

Have you ever been to London?

No, I've never been there but I've been to ...

- **Test your friends' memories.**
  A: Who has been to ...? B: X has.
- **Magic Lingo: Clever "ever"!**

"Has Denis ever been to Denver?" "Yes, he has. He goes there every Easter with Esther."

## THINK AND STORE

**1** **Read and imagine the scene. Make sure you understand everything.**

**Sophie** : Mark, you've travelled a lot. Have you been to Africa?
**Mark** : Yes, I've been to Morocco, to Kenya and to South Africa.
**Sophie** : And you've been to Australia too, haven't you?
**Mark** : Yes, I have.
**Kevin** : And to Japan ? To China?
**Mark** : I've been to Japan, but I've never been to China.

**Rob** : Have you ever been to India?
**Mark** : No, I haven't. I don't know Asia very well .
**Sophie** : What about Europe? Do you know Italy? Spain? Greece?
**Mark** : Yes, I do. I've visited most of Europe, in fact. And I've already lived in France, in Germany, and in Poland.
**Rob** : So, where is home?
**Mark** : Home? Home is where I am. I'm a citizen of the world.

**2** **Pick out the countries Mark has been to. Count them.**

**3** **Open your workbook and learn your lesson step by step.**

### HELP!

**tra**vel

Mo**ro**cco

njə
Kenya

'eɪʒə
**A**sia

dʒ
Ja**pan**

'tʃaɪnə
China

jʊə
Europe

▶ EXERCISES AND GRAMMAR: PAGE 119.

## forget-me-not

**Vérifie que tu sais...** - dire quels pays tu as visités.
- poser la question à tes camarades.

He has already been to Japan, hasn't he?
He has never been to China, has he?

### L'EXPÉRIENCE

*Fait ou non ?*

**Le *present perfect***
(have + *participe passé*)

**Verbes réguliers**
I **have** already liv**ed** in Italy.
He **has** never visit**ed** Milan.

**Verbes irréguliers**
*Le participe passé s'apprend !*
He **has** already **been** to Japan.

**Rappelle-toi :** cinq noms de continents et de pays.
Africa: Morocco, Kenya, South Africa ...
Asia: Japan, China, India ...
Europe: Italy, Spain, Germany, Holland ...

# scene 4

▶ PARLE DE TES EXPÉRIENCES.
▶ PRÉCISE QUAND ELLES ONT EU LIEU.

## 1 SHOW YOU KNOW

- Talk about Mark's travel experiences.
- Ask your teacher what countries (s)he knows.

## 2 SPRING INTO ACTION

- Look and say what you can.
- Listen and discover how to talk about James's experiences.

### YOU AND THE BIG WIDE WORLD!

**Have you ever ...**

| | | Yes | No | Where? When? What? Who with? |
|---|---|---|---|---|
|  | - been abroad? | X | | To France, 1999, to Germany, 2000 and to Italy, 1998. |
|  | - visited a historic building? | X | | Lots! Windsor Castle last month. |
|  | - seen a musical, a play or a ballet? | X | | Yes! I acted in Oliver six months ago. |
|  | - read a novel? | X | | Yes, I've read all the Harry Potters! |
|  | - heard jazz music played live? | | X | But I like Louis Armstrong and the Blues. |
|  | - bought something on the Internet? | X | | First time last week. Cd's and video games. |
|  | - eaten Chinese food? | X | | Restaurant, often. |
| | Japanese food? | X | | Yuck! |
| | haggis? | X | | In Scotland, last year. |
|  | - drunk espresso coffee? | X | | In Italy last August. Too strong. |
| | champagne? | X | | Mum's birthday. Yum, yum! |
| | jasmine tea? | | X | |

**SCORE! 2 points for each "yes".**

**More than 18?** You already know a lot about the world. Well done!
**17 to 12?** You have already done a lot. Life is interesting, isn't it?
**Less than 12?** You are lucky! You still have a lot to discover. Go for it!

- **Now ask your friends and your teacher questions.**

- **Listen: what are Mark's best and worst memories?** WB
- **Answer your teacher's questions.**

T: Name the most beautiful place you have ever seen.
T: When did you go there?

- **Test your friends' memories.**

T: Rome. A: It is the most beautiful city Bruno has ever visited. He went there ...

- **Interview your teacher about her / his experiences.**

▶ PLAY AND LEARN IN YOUR WORKBOOK.
▶ EXERCISES AND GRAMMAR: PAGE 119.

## SAY IT!

ə ɔ:
a**broad**

his**tor**ic

**bu**ilding

tʃaɪ
Chi**nese**

Japa**nese**

**Have you ever ...**

e
- **read?**

3:
- **heard?**

ɔ:
- **bought?**

ʌ
- **drunk?**

## forget-me-not WB

**Vérifie que tu sais...** - parler d'expériences marquantes.
- préciser quand elles ont eu lieu.

Have you ever visited Windsor castle?

Yes, I have.

When did you visit it?

I visited it two months ago.

James **has** already visit**ed** a castle.
He **visited** Windsor Castle two months **ago**.

**Rappelle-toi :** ces participes passés irréguliers.

| | | |
|---|---|---|
| buy → bought [ɔ:] | drink → drunk [ʌ] | eat → eaten |
| hear → heard [3:] | read → read [e] | see → seen |

### PRESENT PERFECT + EVER

*Interroger sur les expériences.*
**Have** you **ever** visit**ed** Rome?
**Have** you **ever been** abroad?

### PRÉTÉRIT

*Raconter.*
*Donner des détails.*
I **visited** London **last week**.
I **was** there **for a week**.
I **saw**, I **bought**, I **ate** ...

### AGO

*Reculer dans le temps en mesurant la distance.*
... a week **ago**.
... two years **ago**.

# Put pen to paper

## 1 Learn to use notes!

**Read the notes a journalist made when he interviewed Mark. Write their conversation.**

## 2 Write it yourself!

**INTERVIEW**

**Choose a real or imaginary celebrity.**

Invent an interview for a teenage magazine.

The celebrity is eccentric and loves exaggerating.

Need help? Workbook!

**a.** Note down your questions, then imagine surprising answers. Ask for more details.

**b.** Write a rough copy, check your punctuation and improve your style.

**c.** Imagine a magazine layout.

# scene 5

**PARS À LA DÉCOUVERTE D'UN MAGAZINE POUR JEUNES.**
- **Dis ce que tu sais.**
- **Prépare-toi.**
- **Lis.**

# Teenage problems

## 1 WHAT DO YOU KNOW? WB

- **What is good and bad for your health?**

## 2 PREPARE TO READ WB

- **Look at these extracts from the next two pages.**

Dear Teen 2000

*Dear Bill*

*So stop worrying and enjoy life!*

**TIPS FROM DR. TEEN**
*(tuyaux)*

In adolescence ...

What should I do?

EATING HABITS

- **Conclude: these extracts come from:**
**a.** a comic strip. **b.** a magazine for young people. **c.** a medical journal.

**Its name is: a.** "Training doctors". **b.** "Teen 2000". **c.** "Bill and Teen".

# scene 5

## 3 SPRING INTO ENGLISH

- **Reading strategies: in each letter and answer, pick out the words relating to the same topic. Then find a title for each letter. We have done the first one for you.**

PROBLEM PAGE • • • • • PROBLEM PAGE • • • • • PROBLEM PAGE

Dear Teen 2000,
All my friends have grown a lot recently but I haven't changed in a year, except for my feet which have become enormous. I'm one of the shortest in my class. Yet my parents are both quite tall. Will I grow soon? **Bill, 13**

*Dear Bill,*
*Your size depends a lot on your genes. If your parents are tall you will probably be tall too. And if your feet are big, it is a good sign, because feet start growing before the rest of the body. You will certainly grow taller in a few months. So stop worrying and enjoy life!*

Dear Teen 2000,
I often quarrel with my parents because they don't want me go out. We've just had the worst fight ever. I'd like to leave home. But where can I go? **Mandy, 14**

*Dear Mandy,*
*You want more freedom but your parents are worried about the dangers you might face. They are strict because they want to protect you. They love you, so try and talk to them. And do not leave home. There is no better place for you.*

Dear Teen 2000,
I am 14. My best friend, Jessica, has just said she doesn't want to be my friend anymore, but I still like her and I am miserable. What should I do? **Melanie, 14**

*Dear Melanie,*
*Separation is always difficult but you can't force somebody to be your friend. Perhaps you should try and talk to her about how you feel. Friendship has its ups and downs and this might only be temporary. But anyway, don't get depressed. Isn't there anybody else you like?*

# TIPS FROM DR. TEEN

## YOUR BODY

In adolescence, your body changes a lot. Help it to develop by exercising regularly and eating healthy food. Washing is essential to get rid of dead skin, dirt and the bacteria responsible for Body Odour (B.O.). And you should also use a deodorant. There are many brands on the market. Try different sorts until you find the right one for you. If your skin is a problem, it might be a good idea to see a doctor because there are lotions and creams that can help.

## EATING HABITS

Girls are always worried about their figures. They want that "top-model look" which is so fashionable, but almost impossible without a constant diet. As a teen-ager, you are growing and it is important to eat enough and well. How much junk food have you eaten today? Try eating fresh fruit and vegetables instead. *Do not diet* without a doctor's advice. It may be dangerous.

**Remember that your body is yours only.**
**Do not accept unpleasant comments from other people about the way you look.**
**And mind what you say to others!**

## 4 LISTEN

- Check! Right or wrong?
- Hygiene over the centuries.

**www.healthfinder@health.org**

# Encore

## 1 REACT

## 2 READ

- **Who is it? (From left to right: Joe, Bob, Jack, Jason, Neil, Bill.)**

**1.** He wants to see the doctor because he has always been too thin and can't get any fatter. Today, like every day, he has already eaten two sandwiches, three packets of chips, four chocolate bars, and a lot more.

**2.** He has been on a diet for three months and he has already lost 20kg, so his clothes are too big for him now. He is very pleased and soon he will be the slimmest in his family.

**3.** This is the great day! He has had his plaster cast for three weeks already, and today the doctor is going to take it off. He will be able to play football again.

**4.** He has come to see the doctor because he has promised his wife that he will stop smoking. He knows it is bad for his health and he finds it more and more difficult to do his body-building.

## 3 LISTEN

- **Oral comprehension.**
  At the doctor's.

- **Phonetics and dictation.**
  An American Record.

# Oral recap.

- **Say the words aloud!**

  **Name five parts of your head!** **Say five adjectives that describe you!** **Name five European countries!**

- **In 30 seconds try to find three words in a line that have the same vowel sound.**

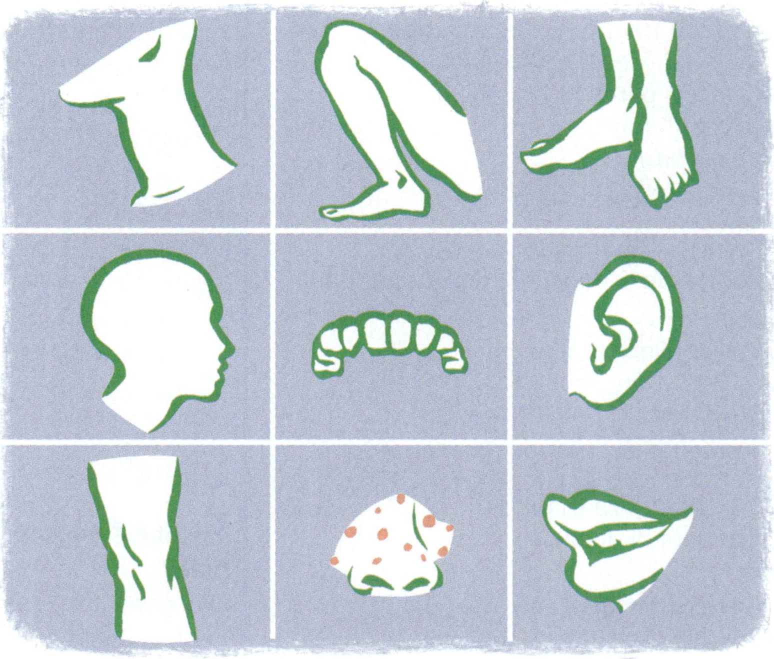

- **Find the odd one out and then make a series for the class.**

uncle - cousin - aunt - nephew - father - niece - friend - grandfather
well-dressed - slim - fit - athletic - strong - sporty - healthy
the prettiest - the most intelligent - the best - the worst - the most beautiful - the kindest - the best-dressed

# Word builder

- **On your pad, classify these words into three columns: verb + -er, adj. + -er, other words.**

composer father explorer stronger river painter fitter brother charmer sportier teacher slimmer discover driver shoulder

- **Conclude: adjective + -er:** **a.** what somebody is or does. **b.** a comparative form.
  **verb + -er:** **a.** what somebody is or does. **b.** a comparative form.

- **Find more words for each category and make tongue-twisters or nonsense rhymes.**

An explorer and a discoverer
Went down a river in Niger
Looking for a tiger!

-er is only a suffix if you can find the base word!

# Grammar

## COMPARER

Tu situes un élément par rapport à un autre. Le second élément sert de référence [de point de comparaison].

London is bigger than Paris.

L'adjectif indique dans quel domaine tu te places :

*big:* la taille *famous:* la célébrité

Tu observes, tu analyses. C'est du travail ! Enfin, tu juges, tu tires une conclusion.

– "c'est au même niveau", "c'est pareil" *(as ... as ...)*
– "ce n'est pas au même niveau" *(not as ... as)*
– "ça dépasse" *(...er / more ... than)*

**• LE COMPARATIF D'ÉGALITÉ**

Les deux éléments sont égaux.
L'équilibre règne dans un domaine. L'anglais le signale par deux *as* identiques.

Rob is as tall as Ben. [jugement : Rob est aussi grand que Ben.]

Tu nies cet équilibre avec *not.*

Rob is not as tall as Ben [contestation : pas aussi grand que ...]

**• LE COMPARATIF DE SUPÉRIORITÉ : *...er / more than.***

Le premier élément est supérieur. Il dépasse.
Il y a donc un déséquilibre.

Sophie is older than her sister. (plus âgée que ...)
She is more artistic than her sister. (plus artiste que ...)

## LE SUPERLATIF

Situe à l'extrêmité et détache du reste : ***the ...est / most.***

– Tout en haut [*"top of the pile"*] = "le plus"

The oldest person in my family.
The most expensive restaurant in London.

– Tout en bas [*"bottom of the pile"*] = "le moins"

The least expensive.

| adjectif | comparatif de supériorité | superlatif |
|---|---|---|
| | **adjectifs "courts"** une syllabe deux syllabes si la dernière lettre est *-y* | |
| tall | taller than | the tallest |
| big | bigger than | the biggest |
| easy | easier than | the easiest |
| | **tous les autres adjectifs** | |
| artistic | more artistic than | the most artistic |

**a.** Trouve les deux points communs entre adjectifs "courts" et adjectifs "longs" au comparatif.
**b.** Fais de même pour le superlatif.

## ENTRAÎNE-TOI

### Setting the scene

**1 Compare-les.**
1. Kirk Douglas / famous / son
2. Jane Birkin / talented / daughter
3. J.F. Kennedy / tall / brothers
4. Charlie Chaplin / funny / daughter
5. Geraldine Chaplin / attractive / father

**2 Compare.**
1. your size / your best friend's
2. your hair / your best friend's
3. your hands / your (grand)mother's
4. your fitness / your gym teacher's
5. your English now / your English last year

### Scene 1

**3 Qui est au sommet, en bien ou en mal ?**
*Ex. :* good actor / family
→ *My cousin is the best actor in my family.*
1. serious / class
2. good tennis player / France
3. slim / family
4. amusing / teacher / school
5. bad cook / family

**4 Construis des phrases vraies pour toi, au comparatif ou au superlatif.**
1. Zidane / famous footballer / in France
2. Ch. Chaplin / funny actor / in the world
3. Johnny Halliday / good singer / his son
4. My ... / talkative / my ...
5. My ... / strong / in the family

### Scene 2

**5 Demande confirmation de ces records français en utilisant un *tag*.**
1. the Mont Blanc (high mountain)
2. Paris (populated city)
3. The Loire (long river)
4. Marseilles (big port)
5. Nice (beautiful city)

**a.** Ce sont les même lettres qui marquent l'idée de supériorité : 'er', (*taller*, *more artistic*). Le deuxième élément est introduit par ***than***. **b.** Ce sont les mêmes lettres qui marquent l'idée d'extrêmité : ***the tallest*** et ***the most*** *artistic*. Les deux types d'adjectifs sont précédés de *the*.

MORE!
▶ EXERCISE BANK, P. 170
▶ GRAMMAR STORE, P. 142

## PRESENT PERFECT AVEC EVER / NEVER

Quelle expérience du monde as-tu ? Cherche bien !

Have you ever been to London?

• **EVER / NEVER**

*Ever* → parcourir sa vie à la recherche d'une expérience particulière.
*Never* → bilan négatif. Jamais fait !

• **L'EXPÉRIENCE :** la vie te l'a donnée ou non.
Maintenant tu l'as (*have*) ou tu ne l'as pas (*have not* / *have never*).

I have been to London. [expérience acquise]
She has never visited a palace. [expérience non acquise]

| ? | + | − |
|---|---|---|
| Have you ever been / visited ...? | I have already been / visited ... | I have never been / visited ... |

**a.** Au *present perfect* quel est le verbe auxiliaire ? Se conjugue-t-il? À quelle forme est le verbe lexical ?
**b.** Quels sont les participes passés de *buy, eat, hear, read, see* ?

## PRESENT PERFECT OU PRÉTÉRIT ?

• **PRESENT PERFECT** : l'important, c'est de l'avoir fait !
Tu donnes la priorité à l'expérience.

I have been to China [Je l'ai fait ! C'est ça qui compte !]
I have not been to Japan. [Je ne l'ai pas fait !]

• **PRÉTÉRIT** : l'important c'est l'histoire (quand, comment ...) :
Tu donnes la priorité aux circonstances, à l'aventure.

I visited China in 1998.

## SITUER EN ARRIÈRE SUR LA LIGNE DU TEMPS

• Tu montres une zone / un point précis dans le passé.

I visited Windsor Castle in 1999 / last week / last Friday.

• Tu recules de 1,2,3 jours / semaines / années, etc.

I visited Windsor Castle 3 days ago. [tu remontes de 3 jours]

Avec *ago*, tu mesures la distance sur l'axe du temps.
Tu lis ce qu'il y a sur le compteur de jours, d'années, etc.
Et comme tu voyages dans le passé, tu utilises le prétérit.

## ENTRAÎNE-TOI

### Scene 3

**6 Dis dans quels continents ce voyageur est déjà allé. Où n'est-il pas allé ?**

**7 Réponds en disant la vérité.**
*Ex. :* Do you know London? → *Yes, I do. I've already been there* ou *No, I don't. I've never been to England / abroad.*

1. Do you know St Malo?
2. Do you know Madrid?
3. Does your best friend know London?
4. Does your mother know Rome?
5. Do your parents know New York?

### Scene 4

**8 Quelle expérience du monde as-tu ? Dis-le, puis pose la question.**
*Ex. :* go to London → *I've already / never been to London. Have you ever been there?*

1. drink Turkish coffee
2. eat haggis
3. read *"Harry Potter"*
4. buy books on the internet
5. see a play in English

**9 Invente des mini-dialogues.**
*Ex. :* good film / see →
*- A: What is the best film you have ever seen?*
*- B: It is ...*
*- A: When did you see it?*
*- B: I saw it ... ago.*

1. good pop concert / hear
2. interesting book / read
3. expensive present / buy
4. cold region / visit
5. bad food / eat

**a.** C'est *have* qui joue le rôle d'auxiliaire. Il se conjugue au présent (d'où l'étiquette „*present perfect*"). Normal ! C'est dans le présent qu'on profite de l'expérience acquise ! Le verbe lexical est au participe passé. Normal ! C'est dans le passé qu'on a acquis l'expérience. **b.** *buy* → *bought* [ɔːt]; *eat* → *eaten*; *hear* → *heard* [ɜː]; *read* → *read* [e]; *see* → *seen*.

# Do-it-yourself

## Make a "have you seen?" puzzle

YOU NEED:
- a postcard or photo of a very famous place
- a postcard-sized photo of a celebrity
- two Bristol cards (12,5 x 20 cm)
- scissors and glue

1 TAKE THE POSTCARD AND CUT IT OUT AS IF TO MAKE A JIGSAW PUZZLE.

2 ON A BRISTOL CARD, GLUE THE PIECES IN ANY POSITION (UPSIDE DOWN, SIDEWAYS, ETC.) TO MAKE IT REALLY HARD TO RECOGNIZE THE PLACE.

3 DO THE SAME WITH THE CELEBRITY.

4 BRING YOUR CARDS TO SCHOOL AND POOL THEM. IN TURN PICK OUT A CARD AND IDENTIFY THE PERSON OR THE PLACE.

5 SCORE ONE POINT EACH TIME YOU HAVE FOUND THE SOLUTION. IF YOU CAN SAY « I'VE ALREADY SEEN / VISITED / MET / HEARD ... », SCORE TWO MORE POINTS.

Find an unusual record on the web.

# Project

## My autobiography

- Make a poster using three photos of yourself: one as a baby, one as a small child, and a recent one.*
- Write a caption under each photo.
- Write your life story with humour. Compare the photos and talk about the changes.
- Finish with a prediction about yourself when you are 20.

* If you prefer, you can create a "would-be you" with photographs from a magazine.

AN AUTOBIOGRAPHY

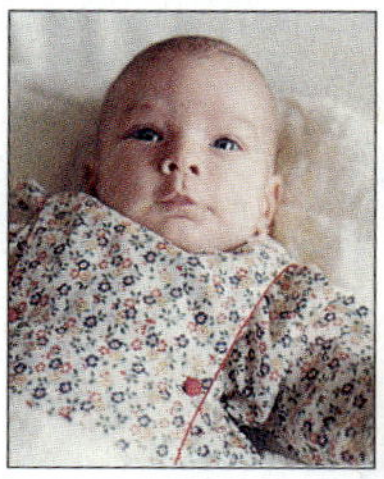

I was born on ... in ...
My parents ...
At the age of ...

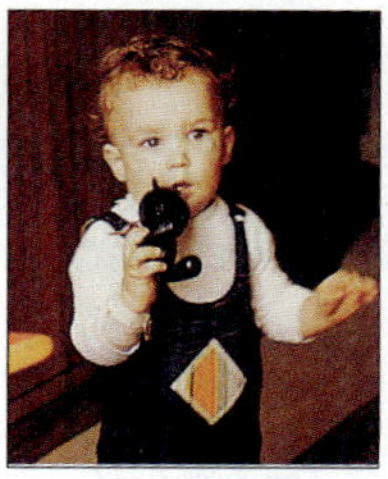

When I was 3 ...

I have changed a lot, haven't I? Now I am the best person ever! I always help when Mum asks. I am never bad-tempered, and when I am 20, I'll ...

## Geographic Alphabet Game

Vote for the funniest autobiography.

1 In small groups, draw five columns on a piece of paper.

2 Write headings for each column as shown in the model.

3 In turn a player says a letter, and everyone writes it in the first column.

4 Now try and complete the grid with geographic names (countries, cities, rivers, mountains) in a limited time (use a timer).

5 Check. Score one for each correctly spelt word and two for a name nobody else has found.

| LETTER | first | last | not first or last | two or more |
|---|---|---|---|---|
| A | Algeria | Campa | France | Canada |
| L | London | | | |
| | | | | |
| | | | | |

web site
www.spring.hachette-education.com

# EPILOGUE

## DANS CE CHAPITRE

### TU VAS T'EXERCER

- à décrire une scène du présent et du passé.
- à dire ce qui se passait à tel ou tel moment.
- à parler de ce que tu sais faire tout(e) seul(e).
- à lire un article de journal.

### TU VAS UTILISER

- *"be + -ing"* au prétérit.
- les pronoms réfléchis (*myself, yourself*, etc.).

### TU VAS REVOIR

- le présent en *"be + -ing"*.
- le prétérit simple.
- le vocabulaire de la ville.

# Partying and parting!

# The robbery

- DÉCRIS UNE SCÈNE.
- PLANTE LE DÉCOR !
- QUE SE PASSAIT-IL À CE MOMENT-LÀ ?

**1** Look and say what you can. Then listen to find out what happened.

**2** a. Listen. What were they doing? What did they see?
b. Talk about your activities at different times.

What were you doing at 6pm yesterday?

I was watching a video.

## forget-me-not

**Vérifie que tu sais...** - décrire une scène du passé.
- dire ce que tu faisais à tel ou tel moment.

Yesterday at 3pm
When the robbery took place } she was cutting Mr Smith's hair.

**Rappelle-toi :** les noms des magasins où tu te rends souvent.

**LE PRÉTÉRIT EN *"BE + -ING"***

**À un moment donné.**

*Voilà comment c'était.*
It was raining.

*Voilà ce qu'on faisait.*
A man was cleaning a window.

**LE PRÉTÉRIT SIMPLE**

*Voilà ce qui est arrivé.*
The police came.
They asked a lot of questions.

# The party

▶ PARLE DE FÊTES ET DE DÉGUISEMENTS.
▶ DIS CE QUE TU SAIS FAIRE SEUL(E).

**3** **Talk about the party. Then listen and find out who is who.**

**4** **a. Listen and report.**

*I always repair my bike myself.*

*He says he always repairs his bike himself.*

**b. Talk about things you made, repaired or decorated yourself. And what about your family? The class asks questions and reacts.**

*I made this bracelet myself.*

*When did you make it?*

*How much did it cost you?*

**5** **Write about the last party you went to. (Where? To celebrate what? Guests? Food? Drink? Fancy-dress? Dancing? Your opinion.)**

## forget-me-not

**Vérifie que tu sais...** - parler de fêtes et de déguisements.
- dire ce que tu sais faire toi-même, ou non.

Ian dressed up **as** Franklin D. Roosevelt, didn't he?
He said (that) he made his mask himself.

**Rappelle-toi :** les pronoms réfléchis.
- singulier : my**self**, your**self**, him**self**, her**self**, it**self**
- pluriel : our**selves**, your**selves**, them**selves**

### CONSTRUCTIONS RÉFLÉCHIES

She is looking at herself.
He is looking at himself.
They are looking at themselves.

I enjoyed myself, *etc.*

**Pas de réfléchi en anglais.**
I **wash** ... "je **me** lave."
I **dress** ... "je **m'**habille."

# A night to remember!

▶ DÉCOUVRE LES CIRCONSTANCES DE L'ARRESTATION DE JIM RICOTTI.

**6** **Read more about Jim Ricotti's arrest.**

**THE LONDON GAZETTE**

Saturday, June 11th

### A BIRTHDAY PARTY TO REMEMBER

## Police arrest dangerous gangster on birthday party boat!

Sherlock Holmes was a gangster! Jim Ricotti after his arrest.
He broke his arm while trying to escape.

Two fourteen-year-old friends, James Wilson and Ian Robinson, were enjoying themselves at their birthday party on the Thames yesterday when it turned into a nightmare.

All of a sudden, at eleven pm, the boat stopped and all the lights went out.

Sophie Macguire, one of the guests, said: "We were all having a great time when suddenly we found ourselves in the dark. It was really scary and the band stopped playing. Then we heard a loudspeaker announce: "Jim Ricotti, we know you are there. The boat is surrounded. There is no escape, so give yourself up."

James Wilson, whose birthday party it was, thought it was a joke! "I had never heard of Jim Ricotti, so I didn't understand and I thought it was a party trick. But when the lights came on again, we heard screams and there was absolute panic. People were running in all directions!"

Another guest said: "I was dancing with a man dressed up as Sherlock Holmes. He was wearing a mask, so I couldn't see who he was, but he was a brilliant dancer!

Then, when the lights went out, he rushed outside and jumped straight into the river! You can imagine how surprised I was!"

Police Inspector Smith from Scotland Yard told our reporter that Jim Ricotti was a notorious gangster wanted by Interpol, and that he could be dangerous. "We arrested him last year but he escaped from Reading Prison and managed to get to California, where Inspector Adams, who is also working on this case, saw him by chance on the beach. After that we were able to follow him from California to London.

Last week he stole some money from an antique shop, and fortunately we managed to arrest his accomplice, Flo Rondo, who told us where he was hiding.

We wanted to catch him red-handed so we followed him all day. From his hotel near Marble Arch, he walked to Buckingham Palace and picked a few pockets during the Changing of the Guard. Then he walked on to Westminster Abbey, where he joined a general tour and picked some more pockets.

Then he went to Saint Paul's

Cathedral by underground and walked to the Tower of London. While he was standing in the queue, he stole three or four more wallets. But he didn't go inside. He took a bus and went to Covent Garden instead. There he bought a Sherlock Holmes costume from a fancy dress shop.

He spent the rest of the afternoon walking from Piccadilly Circus to Trafalgar Square and then back to Westminster.

At around 6.30 pm he stopped in a pub, put on his disguise and arrived all dressed up at 7 pm to get on the party boat. He introduced himself as 'the police officer on duty!' We are now trying to find out why he chose that particular boat and how he heard about the party".

Jim, a 50-year old New Yorker of Italian descent, can speak six languages and is known as "Charlie the linguist". He loves dressing up and changing personalities. He has already escaped from four different prisons, but this time the police are taking no chances!

Inspector Adams from the San Francisco Police was present at the time of the arrest. In fact, by pure coincidence, his son, Ben, was attending the party.

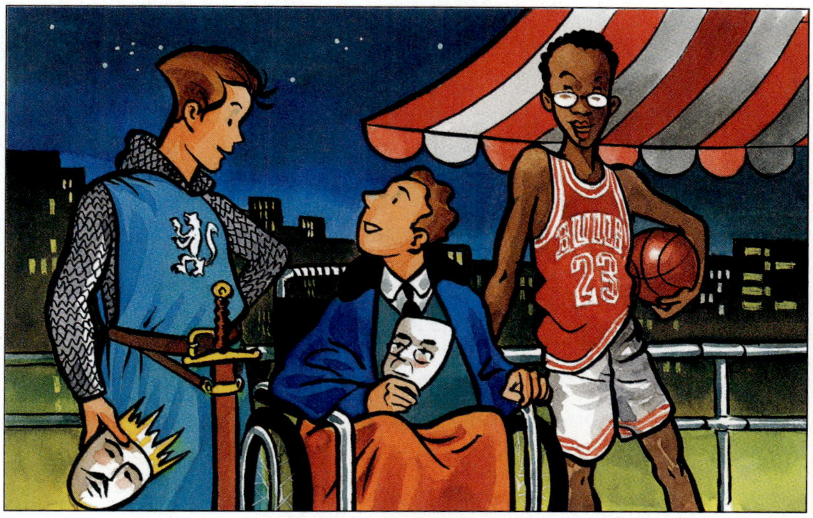
James, Ian and their American friend Ben Adams, who flew over from San Francisco for the party.

**7** **Listen and do the Spring Quiz.**

# Grammar

## LE PRÉTÉRIT AVEC *BE* + *-ING*

Tu conjugues ***be*** au prétérit et tu fixes ***-ing*** au verbe lexical.

| + | ? | − |
|---|---|---|
| I was driving.<br>You were driving. Etc. | Was I driving?<br>Were you driving? Etc. | I am not driving.<br>You were not driving. Etc. |

**a.** Quel verbe est chargé de "lancer" la question ?
**b.** Le verbe lexical change-t-il de forme ?

Le prétérit en *be* + *-ing* : on revoit une scène du passé.

- décrire "comment c'était ce jour-là" [épisode particulier].

  The rain was falling.

- faire un gros plan sur le sujet.

  She was wearing jeans.

- utiliser une action comme toile de fond.

  WE WERE HAVING DINNER
  when we heard an explosion.

[Une chose imprévue survient à l'intérieur d'une scène plus ordinaire]
- prét. *be* + *-ing* pour planter le "décor" : We were having dinner
- prét. simple pour faire surgir l'incident : when we heard ...

- demander des éclaircissements sur des faits acquis.

La question : What were you doing at 6 o'clock?
présuppose ··· [of course you were doing something.]

## LES PRONOMS RÉFLÉCHIS

| singulier : *-self* | pluriel : *-selves* |
|---|---|
| I enjoyed myself | We enjoyed ourselves |
| You enjoyed yourself | You enjoyed yourselves |
| He enjoyed himself<br>She enjoyed herself | They enjoyed themselves |

Compare : 1. He cut the bread. ("il a coupé le pain")
2. He cut himself ("il s'est coupé")

1. *He* dirige l'action sur un élément extérieur *(the bread)*.
2. *He* dirige l'action sur lui-même *(himself)*.

Les réfléchis bloquent l'ouverture sur l'extérieur :

- "retour" ou "repli" sur soi :

She looked at herself in the mirror.

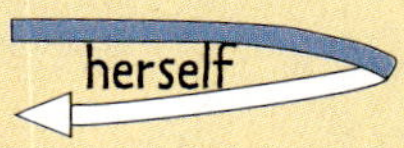


- réalisation sans participation extérieure :

I made the costume myself.
Personne d'autre n'entre dans la réalisation.

myself

## ENTRAÎNE-TOI

### Scene 1

**1 Que faisaient-ils hier aux heures indiquées ? Demande et réponds.**

Ex. : 3 pm / Aliette / work → *What was Aliette doing at 3 pm? She was working.*

1. 10 pm / James / act at the drama club
2. 6 am / Rob / read Harry Potter
3. 11 am / Mrs Wilson / drive to town
4. 1 pm / Mark and James / jog
5. 11.30 am / the Martins / shop

**2 Prétérit simple ou en *be* + *-ing* ?**

1. Yesterday, I (go) to the cinema.
2. I (shop) when I (see) an accident.
3. What ... you (do) at 6 yesterday?
4. Aliette (not see) Mark last week.
5. Rob (phone) Kevin when Ben (arrive).

### Scene 2

**3 Complète par *myself, yourself,* etc.**

1. Rob enjoyed ... at the club yesterday.
2. Sophie made her costume ...
3. The Wilsons prepared the party ...
4. Did you pay for the drink ...?
5. Yes, I paid for it ...
6. You are all wet! Look at ...!

**4 Retrouve la question.**

1. ...? Yes, we did. We had a good time.
2. ...? Yes, and she made her mask too.
3. ...? No, he bought it.
4. ...? I was dancing.
5. ...? No, they weren't. They were reading.

**5 De quel lieu s'agit-il ? Repère-le sur la carte p. 129.**

1. It is the longest church in the world after St Peter's in Rome, and it is the cathedral of London.
2. It is a church where kings and queens are crowned, married and buried.
3. It is an old fortress near the Thames which is now used as a museum.
4. It is the King or Queen's residence.

**a.** *Be* est un auxiliaire, donc *do* est inutile ici. **b.** Une fois que tu as fixé *-ing* à la base, tu n'y touches plus ! *Driving, shopping*, etc. à toutes les personnes ! Aucune différence entre verbes réguliers *(shop)* et irréguliers *(drive)*. *V-ing* pour tout le monde ! Seul l'auxiliaire *be* se conjugue.

# 1
# The Cat and the Fox

One day the fox was walking in the park when he met the most beautiful cat he had ever seen. She was smaller than the fox, but not very much. Her nose was shorter, but not very much. Her tail was thinner, but not very much. All in all she looked enough like the fox for him to fall in love with her.

The cat, however, didn't think much of the fox. She thought that he was a show-off, and anyway, she didn't like redheads. Soon the fox found out where the cat lived, and he hung around every day hoping to see her. Whenever she stepped out of her front door, the fox would spring forward, take her paw, and walk with her. The cat was much too polite to tell the fox to get lost; after all, she had a pedigree.

a redhead: *un rouquin*

to get lost: to go away

The fox liked to talk about himself all the time. "I've got a boat on the river!" he said.

"Indeed?" smiled the cat. "I hate water!"

"I drink whisky with no ice!" smirked the fox. "Would you like some?"

"Gracious no!" said the cat, smiling. "I prefer milk."

"I know a thousand and one tricks," giggled the fox. "How many do you know?"

a trick: *une ruse*

The cat struggled to remember her manners and not use rude words with this silly, bushy-tailed nitwit. "How clever!" she yawned. "I only know *one*."

a nitwit: an idiot

Their walk had taken the two animals into the rough part of town, and they ran into a gang of wolves and bad dogs, all stretched out across the pavement. The cat shot up the nearest tree.

rough: *mal famée*

a wolf: *un loup*

The fox tried his thousand and one tricks. He tried judo and karate, but the gang just punched his nose. He tried telling jokes, but the gang wouldn't listen. It was more fun to kick the fox up into the air. Silliest of all, he tried to fight back and he bit a bad dog's tail. Enraged, the bad dog swung the fox into the air and slammed him against the pavement. Then, tiring of their game, the nasty gang left.

a joke: *une blague*

he bit: *il mordit*

The badly-battered fox looked up into the tree where the cat sat safely. "So what's your one trick?" he snarled.

"I can climb trees," she purred.


From a fable by La Fontaine.

# 2
# The Guard Dog

*L'histoire se passe dans un refuge pour chiens. Parmi les pensionnaires se trouve un petit bâtard dont l'aboiement rauque et puissant fait fuir tous ceux qui l'approchent. S'il n'est pas adopté aujourd'hui, il sera piqué ce soir, ce qui attriste beaucoup la jeune fille qui s'occupe du chenil* (the kennelmaid).

[...] He's the one for the vet today."

"Oh dear," said the kennelmaid. "He's such a lovely little fellow. Dozens of people fell for him, until ..."

a fellow: *un bonhomme*

fell for him: liked him

"... until he opened his mouth," said the manager. "I know. It's a pity, but you can't blame them. In all my long experience of every sort of dog, I've never come across one with such a dreadful voice. [...]

The guard dog ate a hearty breakfast, and was a little surprised when the kennelmaid came to clean out his run, at the fuss she made of him. She cuddled and stroked and kissed him as if she would never see him again.

to cuddle: *câliner*

to stroke: *caresser*

Then he remembered what the smelly old terrier had said.

This is my fourteenth day, he thought. Great! Someone will pick me out today! He sat, waiting for the time when the public were admitted.

[...] No-one even got to smiling at him that morning. Everybody kept as far away as possible from the dreadful sounds issuing from Number 25, and concentrated upon the other inmates. The guard dog was left strictly alone.

inmate: *pensionnaire*

When at last the batch of would-be owners had left, [...] the guard dog sat silent once more. There was a puzzled look on his extremely small and hairy face.

would-be owners: *les propriétaires potentiels*

Can't understand it, he thought. Nobody seems to want a decent guard dog. But if fourteen days was the limit, then they'd jolly well have to find him somewhere to go today. Perhaps the man in the white coat would take him too – he'd seemed a nice sort of chap.

a chap: a man

He watched the door to the kennel block.

It was not the man in the white coat who came in but the kennelmaid with a man with white hair, who walked with a stick with a rubber tip to it.

a stick: *une canne*

"Would you like me to come round with you?" the kennelmaid

said, but he did not answer, so she went away and left him alone.

The old man walked slowly along the row of kennels, looking carefully into each with sharp blue eyes. At last he came to Number 25.

Outside the door, the kennelmaid stood listening, her fingers tightly crossed. But then she heard that fearful noise start up and shook her head sadly.

shook: *passé de* shake, *secouer*

She went back into the kennel block to find the old man squatting on his heels. There was a grin on his face as he looked, apparently totally unmoved, at the howling bawling yowling squalling guard dog.

to squat: *s'accroupir*

a grin: a smile

to howl, to bawl: *hurler*

He levered himself to his feet. "I'll have this little fellow," he said firmly. "He's the boy for me."

"Oh good!" cried the kennelmaid. "He's lovely, don't you think?" But the old man did not answer.

He did not reply later either, when he had paid for the guard dog and the kennelmaid said, "Would you like a box to carry him in?" And in answer to the manager's question, "What are you going to call him?" he only said, "Good afternoon."

light dawned: he understood

Light suddenly dawned on the manager of the Dog's Home. He stood directly in front of the guard dog's new owner so as to be sure of catching his eye, and said deliberately, in a normal tone, "That's some dog you've got there. The worst voice in the world!"

The old man put his hand up to his ear.

"Sorry?" he said. "Didn't catch that. I'm as deaf as a post and I can't be bothered with those hearing-aid things – never been able to get on with them. What did you say?"

deaf as a post: *sourd comme un pot*

"That's some dog you've got there. The best choice in the world!" said the manager very loudly.

The white-haired old man only smiled. [...]

The manager shouted as loudly as he could, "He's a dear little chappie!"

"See that he's really happy?" said the old man. "Of course I will, you needn't worry about that. We'll be as happy as two peas in a pod."

He fondled the puppy's extremely small hairy ears.

to fondle: *caresser*

"Funny," he said. "I fell for him though he wasn't actually what I was looking for. I live all on my own, you see, so really it would have been more sensible to get a guard dog."

sensible: reasonable

## CATS

Cats sleep
Anywhere,
Any table,
Any chair,
Top of piano,
Window ledge,
In the middle,
On the edge,
Open drawer,
Empty shoe,
Anybody's
Lap will do,
Fitted in a
Cardboard box,
In the cupboard
With your frocks.
Anywhere!
They don't care!
Cats sleep
Anywhere.

Eleanor Farjeon

## SNAIL

Snail upon the wall,
Have you got at all
Anything to tell
About your shell?

Only this, my child –
When the wind is wild,
Or when the sun is hot,
It's all I've got.

John Drinkwater

## THE PANCAKE

MIX A PANCAKE,
STIR A PANCAKE,
POP IT IN THE PAN.

FRY THE PANCAKE,
TOSS THE PANCAKE,
CATCH IT IF YOU CAN.

CHRISTINA ROSSETTI

## LONDON TOWN

Which is the way to London Town,
To see the King in his golden crown?
One foot up and one foot down,
That's the way to London Town.

Which is the way to London Town?
Over the hills, across the down;
Over the ridges and over the bridges,
That is the way to London Town.

And what shall I see in London Town?
Many a building old and brown,
Many a real, old-fashioned street
You'll be sure to see in London Town.

# Rhythm and Rhyme

## LAVENDER'S BLUE

Lavender's blue, diddle diddle
Lavender's green,
When I am king, diddle diddle
You shall be queen.

Lavender's green, diddle diddle
Lavender's blue,
You must love me, diddle diddle
'Cause I love you.

Traditional English folksong

## DAISY

Daisy, Daisy, give me your answer do,
I'm half crazy all for the love of you,
It won't be a stylish marriage,
I can't afford a carriage,
But you'll look sweet
Upon the seat
Of a bicycle made for two!

Traditional English folksong

## Auld Lang Syne

Should auld acquaintance be forgot
And never brought to mind?
Should auld acquaintance be forgot
And days of auld lang syne?

*Chorus*
*For auld lang syne, my dear,*
*For auld lang syne*
*We'll tak' a cup o' kindness yet*
*For the sake of auld lang syne.*

Robert Burns

# THE TWELVE DAYS OF CHRISTMAS

On the first day of Christmas,
My true love sent to me,
A partridge in a pear tree.

On the second day of Christmas,
My true love sent to me,
Two turtle doves
And a partridge in a pear tree.

On the third day of Christmas,
My true love sent to me,
Three French hens, two turtle doves,
And a partridge in a pear tree.

On the fourth day of Christmas,
My true love sent to me,
Four calling birds, three French hens, two turtle doves
And a partridge in a pear tree.

5. five gold rings
6. six geese a' laying
7. seven swans a' swimming
8. eight maids a' milking
9. nine ladies dancing
10. ten lords a-leaping
11. eleven pipers piping
12. twelve drummers drumming

Traditional Gaelic folksong

## MOLLY MALONE

IN DUBLIN'S FAIR CITY,
WHERE GIRLS ARE SO PRETTY,
I FIRST SET MY EYES ON SWEET MOLLY MALONE,
AS SHE PUSHED HER WHEELBARROW
THROUGH STREETS BROAD AND NARROW,
CRYING, "COCKLES AND MUSSELS, ALIVE, ALIVE OH!"

CHORUS:
ALIVE, ALIVE OH! ALIVE, ALIVE OH!
CRYING, "COCKLES AND MUSSELS, ALIVE, ALIVE OH!"

NOW SHE WAS A FISHMONGER,
AND SURE TWAS NO WONDER,
FOR SO WERE HER MOTHER AND FATHER BEFORE,
AND THEY EACH WHEELED THEIR BARROW,
THROUGH STREETS BROAD AND NARROW,
CRYING "COCKLES AND MUSSELS, ALIVE, ALIVE OH!"

CHORUS.

SHE DIED OF A FEVER,
AND NO ONE COULD SAVE HER,
AND THAT WAS THE END OF SWEET MOLLY MALONE.
NOW HER GHOST WHEELS HER BARROW,
THROUGH STREETS BROAD AND NARROW,
CRYING, "COCKLES AND MUSSELS, ALIVE, ALIVE OH!"

CHORUS.

TRADITIONAL IRISH FOLKSONG

# Grammar store

## INDEX ALPHABÉTIQUE

# Grammar store

## LA PERSONNE

SINGULIER

PLURIEL

### Le sais-tu ?

- Le **pro-** de **pro**nom signifie "mis à la place de...". Dans **personnel**, il y a l'idée de "personne".

→ Un **pronom personnel**, c'est donc **un mot comme *HE, SHE,* etc. qui remplace un nom de personne.**

### Es-tu sûr d'avoir compris "la personne" ?

- ***I** speak*. La **personne qui parle** est importante. Elle vient en premier. C'est la **1ère personne**.
- ***YOU** listen*. La **personne qui écoute** vient juste après. C'est la **2e personne**.
- ***HE / SHE** does ... is ... has ...* . La **personne dont on parle (toi et moi)** vient en dernier. C'est la **3e personne**.

### As-tu remarqué ?

- ***YOU*** passe partout ! Au singulier et au pluriel ; pour parler à un copain ou au Président !
- ***IT*** est neutre. En latin, *neuter* = "ni l'un ni l'autre".

***It*** représente ce qui n'est **ni du sexe masculin *(HE)*, ni du sexe féminin *(SHE)*** : les choses (puisqu'elles n'ont pas de sexe), les créatures vivantes sans sexe ou de sexe inconnu.

→ ***IT*** est un pronom, mais il n'est pas "personnel". ***IT*** ignore la personne et le sexe.

- ***THEY* rassemble tout le monde** : les hommes, les femmes, les animaux, les choses. Sans discrimination !

# Grammar store

# BE

## "BE" AU PRÉSENT

| AFFIRMATION + | |
|---|---|
| forme pleine | forme contractée |
| I am | I'm |
| You are | You're |
| He<br>She is<br>It | He<br>She 's<br>It |
| We<br>You are<br>They | We<br>You 're<br>They |

### As-tu remarqué ?

- Quand tu parles, tu emploies les **formes contractées** :
  *You're my friend!*
  C'est la première voyelle qui est "avalée". Pour écrire une forme contractée, tu remplaces la voyelle par ':
  *am → 'm are → 're is → 's*
- Tu utilises toujours les **formes pleines** en début et en fin de phrase.
  *Are you French? Yes, I am.*
  *Are they English? Yes, they are.*

| NÉGATION − | | |
|---|---|---|
| forme pleine | forme contractée | |
| I am not | I'm not | I'm not |
| You are not | You're not | You aren't |
| He<br>She is not<br>It | He<br>She 's not<br>It | He<br>She isn't<br>It |
| We<br>You are not<br>They | We<br>You 're not<br>They | We<br>You aren't<br>They |

### Le sais-tu ?

- Au présent, il y a deux manières de contracter la forme − :
  **1.** On contracte ***be*** : *He's not my friend!*
  ***Not*** reste entier et peut être mis en relief.
  **2.** On contracte ***not*** et on le colle : *He isn't.*

### Grammar Quiz

- À la 1ère personne du singulier, il n'y a qu'une manière de contracter. Laquelle ?

| INTERROGATION ? | |
|---|---|
| Positif + | Négatif − |
| Am I? | Aren't I? |
| Are you? | Aren't you? |
| Is he? / she? / it? | Isn't he? / she? / it? |
| Are we? / you? / they? | Aren't we? / you? / they? |

### As-tu remarqué ?

- À la *1ère personne du singulier*, on dit ***Aren't I?*** car on ne peut pas contracter ***am not***.
  *I'm your brother, aren't I?*

### Grammar Booster

- La forme ? − (interro-négative) te permet de former un *tag* à la fin d'une phrase positive +.
  \+ *Ben is American, isn't he?* −
  \+ *You are French, aren't you?* −

## "THERE IS / THERE ARE"

| | Singulier | Pluriel |
|---|---|---|
| + | There is a shop. | There are ... |
| ? | Is there a shop? | Are there ...? |
| − | There is not a shop. | There are ... |

### Le sais-tu ?

- ***There is ...*** permet de dire que quelque chose existe ou se trouve quelque part. *There is a shop in my street.*
- ***Be*** s'accorde en nombre :
  - **une chose à présenter** : *there is ...*
  - **plusieurs choses** : *there are ...*

### Grammar Booster

- Ce n'est pas un hasard si on rencontre *there* (là) dans *there is*. Quand une chose existe, elle se trouve forcément dans un endroit.

# Grammar store

## "BE" AU PRÉTÉRIT

| + | ? | − forme pleine | − forme contractée |
|---|---|---|---|
| I was | Was I? | I was not | I wasn't |
| You were | Were you? | You were not | You weren't |
| He / She / It was | Was he? / she? / it? | He / She / It was not | He / She / It wasn't |
| We / You / They were | Were we? / you? / they? | We / You / They were not | We / You / They weren't |

### Le sais-tu ?

- À l'affirmatif +, pas de forme contractée, mais une voyelle qui s'entend à peine (on la décolore).
*I was* [wəz] *a pretty baby.*
*You were* [wə] *a big baby.*

## "BE" AVEC "BE GOING TO"

| + | ? | − |
|---|---|---|
| I am going to be 12 in May.<br>You are going to be 12 in May.<br>Etc. | Am I going to be ...?<br>Are you going to be ...?<br>Etc. | I am not going to be ...<br>You are not going to be ...<br>Etc. |

### As-tu remarqué ?

- C'est le premier ***be*** qui se conjugue.

### Grammar Booster

- Dans ***be going to***, tu reconnais :
  - ***go*** (idée d'avancer)
  - ***to*** (idée de destination).
  Tu te diriges vers l'événement.

## "BE" AVEC "WILL"

| + | ? | − |
|---|---|---|
| I will be 12 in May.<br>You will be 12 in May. Etc. | Will I be ...?<br>Will you be ...? Etc. | I will not be ...<br>You will not be ... Etc. (won't) |

## "BE" À L'IMPÉRATIF + ADJECTIF

### Ça dit quoi ?

"Je veux (ou je ne veux pas) que tu te comportes comme ça !"

| *Be* + adjectif | *Do not* + *be* + adjectif |
|---|---|
| Be quiet! | Do not be rude! (don't) |

### As-tu remarqué ?

- Il y a des adjectifs comme *quiet, good, rude*, etc. qui décrivent des façons d'être (calme, sage, insolent). À l'impératif, on utilise :
  - ***be*** pour obtenir une certaine attitude.
    *Be quiet!* (Sois sage !)
  - ***don't be*** pour faire cesser une attitude.
    *Don't be rude!* (Ne sois pas grossier !)

## "BE" AVEC "MUST"

| Il le faut. | Il ne faut pas. |
|---|---|
| I<br>You must be quiet.<br>He Etc. | I<br>You must not be rude.<br>He Etc. |

### Grammar Booster

- ***Must*** c'est une **force** qui **pousse vers** *quiet*, etc.
- ***Mustn't*** c'est une **force** qui **tire en arrière** pour éloigner de *noisy, rude*, etc.

# HAVE & HAVE GOT

## "HAVE GOT" AU PRÉSENT

| AFFIRMATION + | |
|---|---|
| forme pleine | forme contractée |
| I / You have got | I / You 've got |
| He / She / It has got | He / She / It 's got |
| We / You / They have got | We / You / They 've got |

**Le sais-tu ?**

- *Have* ne se contracte pas en début et en fin de phrase.
  *Have you got a dog? Yes, I have.*
  *Has she got a cat? Yes, she has.*

Ailleurs, la contraction est possible.
*I've got a dog. She's got a cat.*

Attention au sens ! Ne confonds pas :
*He's got a brother.* 's = ***has***
*He's English.* 's = ***is***

| NÉGATION − | | INTERROGATION ? |
|---|---|---|
| forme pleine | forme contractée | |
| I / You have not got | I / You haven't got | Have I / you got? |
| He / She / It has not got | He / She / It hasn't got | Has he / she / it got? |
| We / You / They have not got | We / You / They haven't got | Have we / you / they got? |

**Le sais-tu ?**

- En anglais américain et parfois anglais britannique, on emploie *have* sans *got*.
  *He has a brother.*

Dans ce cas, *have* travaille avec l'auxiliaire *do*, comme n'importe quel verbe lexical ('ordinaire').
*Does he **have** a brother?*
*No, he doesn't.*

**Grammar Booster**

- Pourquoi dit-on souvent *I've got a dog* en anglais britannique ? À quoi sert *got* ?
  *I've got ...* signifie mot à mot "j'ai obtenu" ou "j'ai reçu" quelque chose.
  Si j'ai un chien, c'est qu'on me l'a donné ou que je l'ai acheté. Il y a forcément une histoire derrière ce chien.
  Tout ce qu'on a maintenant *(have)*, on l'a forcément reçu ou obtenu avant *(got)*.

## "HAVE" AU PRÉTÉRIT

| + | ? | − forme pleine | − forme contractée |
|---|---|---|---|
| I / You / He / Etc. had | Did I / you / he / Etc. have? | I / You / He / Etc. did not have | I / You / He / Etc. didn't have |

**As-tu remarqué ?**

- À la forme +, on se sert du **passé de *have*** → *had*.
- Au formes − et ? c'est **le passé de *do*** → *did*.
- Au passé, il n'y a plus de différence entre 🇬🇧 et 🇺🇸.

# Grammar store

## "HAVE" AU PRÉSENT EN "BE + -ING"

| + | ? | – |
|---|---|---|
| I am having<br>Etc. | Am I having?<br>Etc. | I am not having<br>Etc. |

**As-tu remarqué ?**

- C'est ***be*** qui se conjugue.
- ***Have*** a le sens de "prendre" (un repas, une boisson) ou "organiser" (une fête).
  *She is having breakfast / tea / a party.*

## "HAVE" AVEC "BE GOING TO"

| + | ? | – |
|---|---|---|
| I am going to have<br>You are going to have<br>Etc. | Am I going to have?<br>Are you going to have?<br>Etc. | I am not going to have<br>You are not going to have<br>Etc. |

**Le sais-tu ?**

- Pour former le *"go-future"* :
  *be + going to* + base verbale
- C'est ***be*** qui se conjugue.
  Le reste ne change pas.

## "HAVE" À L'IMPÉRATIF

| + | – |
|---|---|
| Have a hot chocolate! | Don't have a whisky! |

**Le sais-tu ?**

- À l'impératif +, *HAVE* est souvent utilisé pour proposer quelque chose à boire, à manger, etc. Le ton est amical.
  *Have a drink!*
- À l'impératif –, on empêche de ..., ou on retient de ... .
  *Don't have a whisky!*
- Pour vaincre gentiment une résistance, on peut dire :
  *Please don't have ...*

## "HAVE TO" + BASE VERBALE

### au présent

| + | ? | – |
|---|---|---|
| I / you, etc. have to work.<br>He / she has to work. | Do I / you, etc. have to work?<br>Does he / she have to work? | I / you, etc. don't have to work.<br>He / she doesn't have to work. |

### au prétérit

| + | ? | – |
|---|---|---|
| I / you, etc. had to work. | Did I / you, etc. have to work? | I / you, etc. didn't have to work. |

### avec *will*

| + | ? | – |
|---|---|---|
| I / you, etc. will have to work. | Will I / you, etc. have to work? | I / you, etc. won't have to work. |

**Grammar Booster**

Avec ***have to***, il n'y a pas (ou plus) de négociation possible. **On est tenu d'agir.**

- ***Have to*** "enchaîne", "emprisonne" : on n'y échappe pas !
- ***Don't have to*** "brise la chaîne", "libère" : on y échappe !

# Grammar store

## LES VERBES LEXICAUX

### Le sais-tu ?

- Les **verbes lexicaux** sont les verbes "ordinaires" de la langue. On peut expliquer ou traduire leur sens : *walk* "action d'avancer en se tenant debout", "marcher".
- On les appelle **lexicaux** parce qu'ils appartiennent au **lexique** (= la grande réserve de mots de la langue).
- On oppose les **verbes lexicaux** aux **verbes auxiliaires**, comme *BE, HAVE, DO*, qui sont de simples **outils de grammaire**.
- On appelle **base verbale** *(walk)* la forme qui sert de **base** aux autres : *walk + ed → walked*, etc.

## PRÉSENT SIMPLE

| + | ? | − forme pleine | − forme contractée |
|---|---|---|---|
| I / You help | Do I / you help? | I / You do not help | I / You don't help |
| He / She / It help[s] | Do[es] he / she / it help? | He / She / It do[es] not help | He / She / It do[es]n't help |
| We / You / They help | Do we / you / they help? | We / You / They do not help | We / You / They don't help |

N'oublie pas le *s* ou *es* de la troisième personne du singulier, à l'écrit et à l'oral !
- *helps, talks* [s]
- *does, buys* [z]
- *washes* [ɪz]

### Le sais-tu ?

- Avec le **présent simple** le message reste toujours simple :
  "c'est comme ça" : *Birds sing.*
  "c'est vrai" : *I love you.*
  "c'est ce qui se fait" : *He drinks tea.*
  On ne dit rien de plus. *It's a fact!*
- Utile pour parler :
  - **des goûts et des sentiments :** *Ben likes video games.*
  - **des habitudes :** *Sophie gets up at 7.*
  - **de ce qu'on fait ou sait faire dans la vie :** *Brian works in a shop.* *Mary speaks French.*

### As-tu remarqué ?

- Tu as besoin de *do / does* pour ? et −.

## PRÉSENT EN "BE + -ING"

| + | ? | − |
|---|---|---|
| I [am] help[ing] Etc. | [Am] I help[ing]? Etc. | I [am] not help[ing] Etc. |

### Le sais-tu ?

- **Le présent en *"be + -ing"*** peut prendre un sens futur : on a programmé un **déplacement** ou une **réunion**, on s'est **déjà organisé**.
  *I'm leaving tomorrow. I'm flying to America!*
  *We're having a party next week. Are you coming?*
  Ici, on s'est déjà installé dans l'action par l'imagination.
- La projection dans l'avenir est clairement signalée par *tomorrow, next week*, etc.

### Le sais-tu ?

- **Le présent en *"be + -ing"*** fait plonger dans la situation présente et installe tout de suite dans l'action.
- "C'est en ce moment que ça se passe !" *Jim is making a film! I'm helping Dad.*
- "C'est clair qu'on y est (dans l'action) !" *You're cheating!* Évident que tu triches ! *He's not working!* Clair qu'il ne fait rien !

### As-tu remarqué ?

- ***Be*** se conjugue et on accroche *-ing* au verbe lexical : *help → I am helping.*

### Grammar Booster

Le *"be"* de *"be + -ing"* permet de braquer l'attention sur le sujet (regardez-le !) et de lui attribuer une activité *(making a film)*, un comportement *(cheating)*, etc.

# Grammar store

## PRÉTÉRIT SIMPLE

### verbes réguliers

**Ça dit quoi ?**
"Voilà ce qui s'est passé."
"Voilà comment c'était."

| + | ? | – forme pleine | – forme contractée |
|---|---|---|---|
| I<br>You cooked.<br>He<br>Etc. | I<br>Did you cook?<br>he<br>Etc. | I<br>You did not cook.<br>He<br>Etc. | I<br>You didn't cook.<br>He<br>Etc. |

Le *-ed* de la forme affirmative et le *-d* de *did* doivent s'entendre.
*helped* [t] *cleaned* [d] *visited* [ɪd] *did* [d]

**Le sais-tu ?**

- Le **prétérit** permet de parler de ce qui est arrivé AVANT. Tu regardes **en arrière** et tu **racontes** ce qui s'est passé :
  *Brutus killed Caesar.*
  *We cleaned and cooked.*

**As-tu remarqué ?**

- On a besoin de *did* (= prétérit de l'auxiliaire *do*) pour interroger sur le passé ? et pour dire "non, ça n'a pas eu lieu" –.

**Grammar Booster**

- **Prétérit** vient du latin *praeterire*, (dépasser). Logique ! Le passé, c'est ce qu'on a **dépassé** sur la ligne du temps.

### verbes irréguliers

**Le sais-tu ?**

- Normalement, on forme le prétérit + en suivant la **règle** : **base verbale + *-ed*** : *cleaned, cooked, killed*, etc.
- Un verbe qui suit cette règle est **régulier**. Un verbe qui ne la suit pas est **irrégulier**. Il prend une autre forme.

| | |
|---|---|
| be → was / were | have → had |
| break → broke | hide → hid |
| buy → bought | make → made |
| come → came | ride → rode |
| do → did | see → saw |
| drink → drank | sleep → slept |
| drive → drove | speak → spoke |
| eat → ate | steal → stole |
| find → found | swim → swam |
| get → got | take → took |
| go → went | write → wrote |

**As-tu remarqué ?**

- Ces verbes ne sont pas nombreux mais **très utiles**. Ils décrivent des actions **ordinaires**, qui font partie de la vie de tous les jours.
- Tu peux les apprendre par "familles" comme *drove, rode, spoke, stole*, qui partagent le son [əʊ].

| + même forme irrégulière à toutes les personnes | ? auxiliaire *did* (passé de *do*) suivi de la base verbale | – forme pleine | – forme contractée |
|---|---|---|---|
| I<br>You went<br>He<br>Etc. | I<br>Did you go?<br>he<br>Etc. | I<br>You did not go<br>He<br>Etc. | I<br>You didn't go<br>He<br>Etc. |

# Grammar store

## LES VERBES LEXICAUX (suite)

### PRÉTÉRIT SIMPLE ET REPÉRAGES

**Montrer une période ou un moment dans le passé.**

**Reculer de 1, 2, 3 ... jours / semaines / années, etc.**

"When did you see *Hamlet*?" "3 years ago, in Stratford."

**As-tu remarqué ?**

- Au **prétérit**, on donne la priorité à l'histoire. Qui a fait quoi ?
  *On Saturday, I went to London with a friend.*
- Pour situer un événement **en arrière sur la ligne du temps**, on peut :
  - préciser le moment :
    *When? In 1999.*
  - calculer la "distance" en jours / mois, etc.
    *How long ago? 3 days / months ago.*

### LE PRÉTÉRIT AVEC "BE + -ING"

| + | ? | – |
|---|---|---|
| I was driving.<br>You were driving.<br>He<br>She was driving.<br>It Etc. | Was I driving?<br>Were you driving?<br>he<br>Was she driving?<br>it Etc. | I was not driving.<br>You were not driving.<br>He<br>She was not driving.<br>It Etc. |

**Le sais-tu ?**

- On se replonge dans une scène du passé. À un moment donné :
  – voilà comment c'était ... *It was raining ...*
  – voilà ce qu'on faisait ... *I was driving my car ...*
- Dans ce "décor", un événement survint ...
  *... when I heard an explosion.* [prétérit simple]

**As-tu remarqué ?**

- ***Be*** est ici un **verbe auxiliaire** (du latin *auxilium* = aide, secours).
  – *Be* porte la marque du **temps** :
  *was* ... ou *were* ... = passé / prétérit
  – *Be* porte la négation : *was **not** ..., were **not** ...* (wasn't, weren't)
  – *Be* lance l'interrogation :
  *Was I ...? Were you ...?* Etc.
- Le marqueur ***-ing*** est "accroché" au verbe lexical : *drive* → ***driving***.
  Ici, pas de différence entre verbes "réguliers" et "irréguliers" : **V-ing**.

### PRESENT PERFECT + "EVER / NEVER / ALREADY"

| ? | + | – |
|---|---|---|
| Have you ever been to London?<br>Has she ever been to London? | I have already been to London.<br>She has already been to London. | I have never been to London.<br>She has never been to London. |

**As-tu remarqué ?**

- Le ***present perfect*** s'emploie avec ***ever*** pour interroger quelqu'un sur son expérience du monde :
  *Have you ever been to ...? Have you ever visited ...?*
- ***Ever*** est là pour dire "cherche bien partout" !
- ***Never*** signale qu'on a cherché ou parcouru sans trouver.
  *I have never been to ...* : "jamais fait", "non vécu".
- ***Already*** indique que c'est déjà fait :
  *I have already been to ...* : "expérience déjà vécue".

**Le sais-tu ?**

- Forme : ***have*** au prés. + participe passé (p.p.)
- p.p. des verbes réguliers : on ajoute ***-ed***.
  *visit → visited* *live → lived*
- p.p. des verbes irréguliers : ***-en, -t / d***, etc.

| | | | |
|---|---|---|---|
| *be* | → *been* | *eat* | → *eaten* |
| *buy* | → *bought* [ɔː] | *hear* | → *heard* [ɜː] |
| *drink* | → *drunk* [ʌ] | *read* [iː] | → *read* [e] |
| *cut* | → *cut* | *see* | → *seen* |

**Grammar Booster**

Il y a plusieurs façons de répondre à des questions du type *Have you ever been to Japan?*

- Réponse courte : reprise de ***have***.
  + *Yes, I have.* – *No, I haven't.*
- Réponse détaillée : au **prétérit**.
  On raconte, on donne des précisions.
  *Yes, I went to Japan in 1998 and visited Kyoto.*

# Grammar store

## "BE GOING TO"

### the "*go*-future"

**Ça dit quoi ?**
"Ça va arriver."
"C'est bien parti pour se faire."

| + | ? | – |
|---|---|---|
| I am going to fall. *(tomber)*<br>You are going to fall.<br>Etc. | Am I going to fall?<br>Are you going to fall?<br>Etc. | I am not going to fall.<br>You are not going to fall.<br>Etc. |

**Grammar Booster**

- Dans ***be going to***, tu reconnais *go* (idée d'avancer) et *to* (idée de destination). On se dirige déjà (*going*) vers l'action (*to*).

**As-tu remarqué ?**

- Dans ***be going to***, c'est ***be*** qui se conjugue. Le reste ne change pas.

**Le sais-tu ?**

- Avec ***be going to*** **... l'avenir est en route**. On s'y **prépare**.
  On prédit que...
  On prévoit que...

## "WILL"

| Sûr que ça se fera ! | Est-ce que ça se fera ? | Sûr que ça ne se fera pas ! |
|---|---|---|
| I<br>You will write.<br>He ('ll) Etc. | I<br>Will you write?<br>He Etc. | I<br>You will not write.<br>He (won't) Etc. |

**Grammar Booster**

- Avec ***will***, on prend position sur l'avenir. Réalisation garantie !
*I will write to you when I arrive* : "je m'engage à ..." → "Compte dessus."
*James will be 14 next month* : "je le sais ..." → "Aucun doute permis."
- ***Will* fait voir** ce qui se fera, d'un seul coup. Le travail de préparation de l'avenir n'est pas marqué, même s'il existe (≠ ***be going to***). *Will* est donc utile pour se "porter volontaire". La décision semble naturelle et spontanée. *I'll help you. I'll fix it for you.*

**As-tu remarqué ?**

⚠ Pas de *-s* à la 3$^{e}$ personne.
*James will be 14 next week.*

**Le sais-tu ?**

- ***Will*** est un **auxiliaire**. C'est donc lui qui "assure" la négation, l'interrogation, les réponses et les *tags*.
  *Will you be home tonight?*
  *Yes, I will." "No, I won't.*
  *You won't cry, will you?*
- ***Will*** est un **modal** : l'événement futur est présenté sur le **mode** du "sûr et certain".

## "MAY / MIGHT"

| Peut-être que ... ... ça se fera. | ... ça ne se fera pas. |
|---|---|
| I, you, etc. may go to Los Angeles. | I, you, etc. may not go to L.A. |
| **Il y a une petite chance pour que ... ... ça se fasse.** | **... ça ne se fasse pas.** |
| I, you, etc. might go to Los Angeles. | I, you, etc. might not go to L.A. |

**Grammar Booster**

Avec *may* et *might*, on n'est jamais complètement sûr que ça se fera. On ne peut rien garantir !

- Un obstacle peut surgir et gêner l'action : incident, changement de programme, etc. donc pas de voyage à L.A. !
- Une bifurcation (un "embranchement") peut mener ailleurs, vers une autre action : vacances à Miami, donc pas de L.A. !

**As-tu remarqué ?**

- ***May*** est suivi de la base verbale.
- ***May*** et ***might*** sont des modaux : l'événement futur est présenté sur le **mode** du possible.
  *I may go to ...*
  "Il est possible que j'aille à ..."

**Grammar Booster**

Techniquement, *might* est la forme passée de *may*. Ici, le passé sert à faire reculer l'observateur. Comme il est plus loin "en arrière", il voit moins bien l'avenir. Il est donc moins sûr du futur !

# Grammar store

## L'IMPÉRATIF

**Ça dit quoi ?**
"Je veux (ou je ne veux pas) que tu fasses ça !"

| ordre positif + | ordre négatif − |
|---|---|
| Look! | Don't look! |

**Grammar Booster**
- **Impératif** et **empereur** : du latin *imperare* = commander.

**As-tu remarqué ?**
- Je nomme simplement la chose que tu dois **faire** *(Look!)* ou ne **pas faire** *(Don't look!)*.
Pour ça, j'utilise la **base verbale**. C'est du **sens concentré** ! C'est court, c'est clair, ça claque !

## "LET'S ..."

| On veut entraîner les autres. | *Tag* ajouté pour persuader. |
|---|---|
| Let's go to the movies. | Let's go to the movies, shall we? |

**Grammar Booster**
On veut être suivi, sans forcer. Alors on "tire" juste un peu pour "entraîner".

| Proposer un service "Veux-tu que ... ?" | Suggérer une activité collective "Êtes-vous d'accord pour ... ?" |
|---|---|
| Shall I open the window? | Shall we watch a video? |

**Le sais-tu ?**
- *Let's* est suivi de la **base verbale**.
*Let's* **go**. *Let's* **eat** *now.*
- *Let's* [lets] est la contraction de *let us*.

**As-tu remarqué ?**
- On emploie la base verbale après *shall*.
- Ces questions sont des **ouvertures**. Elles invitent les autres à décider *(Shall I ...?)* ou à donner leur avis *(Shall we ...?)*. Réponse positive attendue.

## "MUST"

| Il le faut<br>On pousse vers l'action.<br>On met la pression pour... | Il ne faut pas<br>On éloigne de l'action.<br>On met la pression contre... |
|---|---|
| I, You, etc. must cut your hair. | I, You, etc. must not cut your hair. |

**As-tu remarqué ?**
La pression, on la met en direct ! *Must* appartient donc au présent. Pour parler d'une contrainte passée ou future, tu emploies *had to* et *will have to* ... (voir p. 147).
*He had to cut his hair* : "il le fallait" ou "il a fallu".
*He will have to cut his hair* : "il le faudra".

**Grammar Booster**
- On appelle souvent ***can, could, may, might, shall, should, will*** et ***must*** des **modaux**.
Pourquoi ? Parce qu'ils présentent les faits sur le **mode** :
- du "certain" : *I will be 12.*
- du "probable" : *He may come.*
- du "possible" : *Dad can fix it.*
- du "nécessaire" : *You must help me!*

## "SHOULD"

| Conseiller, suggérer |
|---|
| You, he, etc. should see a doctor. |
| **Déconseiller, reprocher** |
| You, he, etc. should not eat too much chocolate. |

shouldn't

**As-tu remarqué ?**
- Avec ***should***, on "force" moins qu'avec ***must***. Pourquoi ?
– On veut éviter de "mettre trop la pression", par politesse ou par délicatesse.
– On sait qu'on est aidé par la loi, le bon sens, etc. qui "poussent" aussi vers l'action.

# Grammar store

## "CAN"

| C'est permis. C'est possible. | Permis ou non ? Possible ou non ? | Pas permis. Pas possible. |
|---|---|---|
| I<br>You can eat it.<br>He<br>Etc. | I<br>Can you eat it?<br>he<br>Etc. | I<br>You cannot eat it.<br>He<br>Etc. (can't) |

### Grammar Booster

L'action est au bout du chemin !

- *Can* dit que **"la voix est libre"**. On circule sans problème.
- *Can't* dit qu'il y a une **"barrière"** en travers de la route. On est bloqué !

## V1 (SENTIMENT, ATTITUDE) + V2+ -ING

Ian enjoys listening to music.
V1 V2

Deux verbes se suivent : V1 V2 + *-ing*.
Ils se complètent mais ne sont pas sur le même plan.

V1 : plan du sentiment (enjoy, love, like, hate, prefer) porte la marque du temps (présent, passé)

V2 : plan de l'action (listen, walk), porte le marqueur *-ing*

Avec *-ing*, le verbe et les compléments forment un bloc de sens et occupent la place d'un nom.

I like { computers. / surfing the net.

### Grammar Booster

- Avec *-ing*, le verbe et les compléments forment un bloc de sens.

*listening to music*

Ce bloc fait penser à un nom :

*I like { jazz. / listening to music.*

L'activité décrite forme un tout !

## LES "TAGS"

| On affirme. + | Question tag |
|---|---|
| You are American, | aren't you? |
| He has a dog, | hasn't he? |
| She lives here, | doesn't she? Etc. |

| On affirme. − | Question tag |
|---|---|
| You can't swim, | can you? |
| He doesn't live here, | does he? |
| He didn't come, | did he? Etc. |

| On veut entraîner les autres. | Tag |
|---|---|
| Let's go to Disneyland, | shall we? |

### As-tu remarqué ?

- Dans le *tag*, on reprend ***be, have*** ou l'**auxiliaire modal** utilisé dans le corps de la phrase.
  *You have a dog, haven't you?*
- S'il n'y a que le verbe lexical, c'est ***do*** qui est employé.
  *You live here, don't you?*
  *She lives here, doesn't she?*
- Le *tag* est une image **rétrécie** et **inversée** de la phrase.
  *They know Steven, don't they?* (+ / −)
  *They don't know Steven, do they?* (− / +)

### Le sais-tu ?

- Les *tags* sont des petites questions qu'on ajoute à la fin d'une phrase pour **encourager le dialogue** ["qu'en penses-tu ?"] ou **signaler un manque d'assurance** ["dis-moi si je me trompe"].
- *Tag* au sens de "peintures sur les murs" se dit *graffiti*.

# Grammar store

## LES PRONOMS PERSONNELS

| personne | sujet | | complément |
|---|---|---|---|
| 1ère sing. | I | → | me |
| 2e sing. | you | → | you |
| | he | → | him |
| 3e sing. | she | → | her |
| | it | → | it |
| 1ère plur. | we | → | us |
| 2e plur. | you | → | you |
| 3e plur. | they | → | them |

### Grammar Quiz

- Pourquoi dit-on 'pronom personnel' ?
- Pourquoi classer les 'personnes' ?
- Pourquoi ***it*** n'est pas vraiment 'personnel' ?
- Est-ce que ***they*** accueille tout le monde ?

*Pour le savoir, va à la page 143, rubrique "la personne".*

⚠ Attention à la place du pronom complément.

*I like him / her.* *I like them.*

*Je l'aime.* *Je les aime.*

## LES PRONOMS RÉFLÉCHIS

| SINGULIER : *-self* | PLURIEL : *-selves* |
|---|---|
| I cut myself. | We cut ourselves. |
| You cut yourself. | You cut yourselves. |
| He cut himself.<br>She cut herself. | They cut themselves. |

### Grammar Booster

On ne sort pas de soi [*-self*]. Pas d'ouverture sur l'extérieur !

- On s'intéresse à soi-même : *She looked at herself.*
- On se débrouille seul : *I made the mask myself.*

### As-tu remarqué ?

- Souvent, le sujet dirige l'action vers l'extérieur :
  *He cut the bread yesterday. He → bread*
  Avec les réfléchis, l'action part du sujet puis revient à lui :
  *He cut himself : il s'est coupé.*

### Le sais-tu ?

*I enjoyed myself*: "je me suis bien amusé".

⚠ *I wash every day:* "je me lave". Pas de réfléchi.

## LE NOM

### LE PLURIEL DES NOMS

| Type de nom | Pluriel |
|---|---|
| Choses qui se comptent.<br> | books [s]<br>dogs [z]<br>glasses [ɪz] |
| Choses qui ne se comptent pas.<br> | |

⚠ Il y a quelques pluriels qui ne suivent pas la règle.

*man → men* *woman → women*

*child → children* *tooth → teeth* foot → *feet*

### Le sais-tu ?

- Le *-s* du pluriel est réservé aux choses qui se comptent à l'unité : *two books; five days; ten stories.*

  ⚠ Il y a des choses qu'on refuse de compter à l'unité, comme *hair* (= les cheveux). On les traite "en bloc", comme une masse compacte : *beautiful hair* (une belle chevelure = de beaux cheveux).

### As-tu remarqué ?

- Le **marqueur du pluriel** *-S* s'écrit *-s (books)*, parfois *-es (glasses; boxes)*. Il doit toujours s'entendre :
  *books* [s] *dogs* [z] *glasses* [ɪz]

### Grammar Booster

- Quand on ne compte pas à l'unité, c'est qu'on donne priorité à la matière, à la substance : *milk* [le lait, substance liquide]; *wood* [le bois-matériau]; *fruit* [le fruit-aliment]; *information* [l'info qui se consomme].

# Grammar store

## LES DÉTERMINANTS DU NOM

### ARTICLES, DÉTERMINANT ZÉRO (Ø)

| | singulier | pluriel |
|---|---|---|
| article A(N) | a / an | Ø...-s |
| article THE | the | the |

**Le sais-tu ?**

- ***A*** devient ***AN*** devant un son voyelle ou un "h" muet : *an apple; an hour.*
- Au pluriel, ***A(N)*** se transforme en ***Ø...-s*** : *I like Ø apples. I have Ø apples for breakfast.*

**Grammar Booster**

- *A(N)* provient de *ONE*. Voilà pourquoi **il ne peut pas s'employer avec un nom pluriel** : *Give me* ***a*** ***pen! Give me*** ***pens!*** En français aussi, UN = 1.
- *THE* vient de *THAT*. Voilà pourquoi on l'utilise souvent pour renvoyer à un objet précis déjà repéré dans la situation : *I want* ***the*** *blue shirt.*

**As-tu bien compris ?**

- Au singulier, on se sert du **déterminant zéro (Ø)** pour **nommer directement** la substance : *I like Ø milk.* (L'important, c'est la boisson.)
- On s'en sert aussi pour nommer directement les gens *(Ø Rob)*, les langues *(Ø English)*, les repas *(Ø breakfast)*.

### "THIS" ET "THAT"

| singulier | pluriel |
|---|---|
| this book | these books |
| that book | those books |

**Grammar Booster**

- Quand ***this*** et ***that*** travaillent ensemble, ***this*** "ouvre", ***that*** "ferme".
  *This is Flo, and that's Jim.*

**Le sais-tu ?**

- ***This*** et ***that*** permettent **d'attirer l'attention** sur quelqu'un ou quelque chose.
  *This is your Captain speaking. Did you hear that?*
  Parfois, ils sont accompagnés d'un geste qui **montre** : *Give me this book.*
  C'est ce geste qui rend ***this*** et ***that*** **démonstratifs**.
- Pour répondre à une question avec *this* ou *that*, on utilise ***it***.
  *"Who's this?" "**It**'s Ben." "What's that?" "**It**'s a computer."*

⚠ En anglais, on est obligé de marquer la différence entre :
- ce qui est **tout près de soi** *(this)* et ce qui est **plus éloigné** *(that)*.
- un **fait nouveau / inattendu** *(this)* et un **fait connu / attendu** *(that)*.

C'est plus strict qu'en français, où "ce" et "ça" passent partout !

### LES DÉTERMINANTS PERSONNELS (POSSESSIFS)

| QUI | POSSÈDE | QUOI ? |
|---|---|---|
| **singulier** | | |
| I | MY | shoe(s) |
| you | YOUR | shoe(s) |
| he / she | HIS / HER | shoe(s) |
| **pluriel** | | |
| we | OUR | shoe(s) |
| you | YOUR | shoe(s) |
| they | THEIR | shoe(s) |

⚠ 

***His*** *shoes are red.* ***Her*** *shoes are blue.*

**As-tu remarqué ?**

- À chaque pronom **personnel *(I, you...)*** correspond un déterminant **personnel (possessif)** (ex. *I* → *MY*).
  Pour les retenir, aide-toi :
  - des similarités de sons : *I* [aɪ] *MY* [aɪ]
  - des lettres (*HE* → *HIS*, *SHE* → *HER*, *YOU* → *YOUR*).

**Grammar Booster**

- *MY, YOUR*, etc. **limitent** le mot *shoe* : on parle de chaussures particulières, qui appartiennent à une personne particulière. Ce sont donc des **déterminants** (du latin *determino*, "limiter").
- *My* et *YOUR* **relient** *shoe* à une personne : ils sont donc **personnels**.
- *MY, YOUR*, etc. sont souvent appelés des **possessifs** car la personne possède la chose : *MY shoes.* Mais ce n'est pas toujours le cas. Je dis *MY mother*, mais je ne suis pas propriétaire de ma mère ! Il est plus juste de dire que ma mère et moi on est **liés de très près**.

# Grammar store

## DÉTERMINER AVEC UN NOM : LE GÉNITIF

Whose house? Mark['s] house. Whose sister? Sophie['s] sister. Whose dog? Jame['s] dog.

Mark / Sophie / James ●——['S]——● house / sister / dog

### Grammar Booster

Tu utilises *Mark* pour **déterminer** (limiter + identifier) *house*. Tu parles d'une maison précise et tu la **repères** par rapport à quelqu'un. 's marque ce **repérage**.

### Le sais-tu ?

- Le 's crée un lien très fort entre *Mark* et sa maison, *Sophie* et sa sœur, *James* et son chien. Il doit toujours s'entendre :

  *Mark's* [s] (sssss) *Sophie's* [z] (zzzz) *James's* [ɪz] (ɪzzz)

- En français le lien est créé par "de".
- Le premier nom est un **nom de personne** (parfois d'**animal**, de **ville** ou de **pays**).
- Tu emploies ***whose?*** quand tu ne sais pas à qui *(who?)* rattacher *('s)* la chose : *Whose book is this?*

# LES ADJECTIFS

She's got short curly black hair.
↓ taille ↓ forme ↓ couleur

### Grammar Booster

- Les **adjectifs épithètes** sont des "capsules d'information" qu'on injecte directement dans le nom. Ils permettent de faire des "piqûres de sens".
- Certains précisent la taille (big), la forme (curly), la couleur (green), l'origine (French).
- D'autres expriment une opinion (beautiful).
- En règle générale, on va du plus "subjectif" au plus "objectif" : *a beautiful French* ***car***.

### As-tu remarqué ?

- Tous les **adjectifs** sont **invariables**. On ne marque ni le pluriel, ni le féminin.

### Le sais-tu ?

- Quand l'adjectif est **directement accroché au nom**, sa fonction est **épithète** (du grec *epitheton* : 'mot qui est ajouté') et il se met toujours **devant** : *black hair; big eyes.*
- Si plusieurs épithètes se "bousculent" devant le nom, on les place dans l'ordre suivant :
  1. taille 2. forme 3. couleur 4. nationalité
- Quand l'adjectif est accroché au nom à l'aide de *be*, sa fonction est **attribut**. Dans *the house is big*, on "attribue" à *house* la propriété *big*.

## COMPARATIF D'ÉGALITÉ

| Au même niveau. Équilibré ! | | Pas au même niveau. Équilibre rejeté ! | |
|---|---|---|---|
| ... as good as ... | ... as famous as ... | ... not as good as ... | ... not as famous as ... |

## COMPARATIF DE SUPÉRIORITÉ ET SUPERLATIF

| adjectif | comparatif de supériorité | superlatif |
|---|---|---|
| | **adjectifs "courts"** une syllabe deux syllabes si dernière lettre -y | |
| tall | taller than | the tallest |
| big | bigger than | the biggest |
| easy | easier than | the easiest |
| | **tous les autres adjectifs** | |
| artistic | more artistic than | the most artistic |

### As-tu remarqué ?

- La lettre *"y"* se transforme en *"i"* quand on ajoute *-er* ou *-est* : *easy* → *easier than, the easiest*

### Le sais-tu ?

- Au comparatif on "compare" deux éléments. L'un dépasse l'autre : *Rob is taller than Ben.*
- Au superlatif, on détache un élément de tout le reste et on le place à l'extrémité + ou –.

  *The highest mountain in the world.*

# Grammar store

## LES QUANTIFIEURS INDÉFINIS

### MUCH / MANY, A LITTLE / A FEW, TOO / NOT ENOUGH

| type de nom et méthode de quantification | une petite quantité | pas assez | pas beaucoup | beaucoup | trop = excessif | combien ? |
|---|---|---|---|---|---|---|
| Ça se compte à l'unité comme des coquillages 1, 2, 3…  | **a few** shells books | **not enough** shells books milk butter patience | **not many** shells books | **a lot of** shells books milk butter patience | **too many** shells books | **how many?** shells books |
| Ça se mesure "au volume", ça se pèse "en bloc", comme de la matière liquide *(milk)*, solide *(butter)*, ou abstraite *(patience)*. 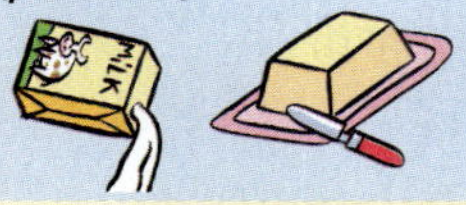 | **a little** milk butter patience | | **not much** milk butter patience | | **too much** milk butter patience | **how much?** milk butter patience |

**As-tu remarqué ?**

- On appelle **quantifieurs** les mots qui indiquent la **quantité** ou le **nombre**. Si le nombre est précis, le quantifieur est **défini** : *two books.* Si le nombre est imprécis, le quantifieur est **indéfini** : *a few books, a little milk.*

⚠ Pour demander le prix : *How much is it?* (sing.) *How much are they?* (plur.)

### SOME & ANY

| | + | ? | − |
|---|---|---|---|
| some | **Il y en a, c'est sûr.** Je le dis. There is some coffee. | **Il y en a, c'est sûr.** J'en propose. Do you want some coffee? J'en demande. Can I have some sugar? | |
| any | | **Il y en a peut-être.** Je me renseigne. Is there any coffee? | **Il n'y en a pas.** Je le dis. There isn't any coffee. |

**Grammar Booster**

- ***Some*** installe dans la réalité. C'est du solide ! *I have some questions for you.*
- ***Any*** projette une image. C'est du virtuel ! *Any questions?*
  - S'il y en a, l'image devient réalité : *Yes, I have a question. I want to know …*
  - S'il n'y en a pas, l'image reste une simple image : *No, there aren't any.*

**As-tu remarqué ?**

- ***Some*** et ***any*** parlent de **quantité** sans la préciser. Ce sont des quantifieurs indéfinis. Ils sont compatibles avec tous les noms communs, donc "passe-partout".

**Le sais-tu ?**

- Le **déterminant Ø (zéro)** permet de **nommer** la substance sans faire allusion à la quantité.
  *Ø Tea or Ø coffee?*
  L'important ici, c'est le type de boisson.

# Grammar store

## LES MOTS INTERROGATIFS

### As-tu remarqué ?

- *Who? What? Where? When?* partagent *wh-?* Ce n'est pas un hasard ! Le message de base est toujours le même ! "Il me manque une information : donne-la moi !" Cette information concerne : l'identité *(who?)*, l'endroit *(where?)*, le moment *(when?)*, etc.

### Le sais-tu ?

- *How?* fait lui aussi partie des **mots en** ***wh-?*** Il s'utilise beaucoup dans des expressions toutes faites comme : *How old?* (Quel âge?) *How tall?* (Quelle taille?) *How many?* (Combien?).

⚠ *wh-* se prononce [**w**] dans *what, when, where* et [**h**] dans *who, how*.

| mot interrogatif | tu cherches une information précise sur ... | exemple |
|---|---|---|
| Who? | une personne | Who is that man? |
| What? | une chose | What is your name? |
| What colour? | la couleur | What colour is your car? |
| What ... doing? | une activité | What are you doing? |
| What time? | l'heure | What time is it? |
| Where? | un lieu | Where do you live? |
| Where ... from? | le pays / la ville d'origine | Where do you come from? |
| When? | le moment | When do you get up in the morning? |
| Whose + nom? | le possesseur | Whose bag is this? |
| How high? | la hauteur | How high is Mount Everest? |
| How old? | l'âge | How old are you? |
| How many? | le nombre / la quantité | How many CDs have you got? |
| How much? | le prix / la quantité | How much tea is there? |
| How tall? | la taille | How tall are you? |
| How well? | la compétence | How well can you swim? |
| How often? | la fréquence | How often do you go shopping? |

### Grammar Booster

- ***How many?*** et ***How much?*** (Combien ?) contiennent ***many*** (un grand nombre de ...) et ***much*** (une grande quantité de ...). On ne sait pas encore le nombre exact, alors on est prudent : on prévoit large !

# Grammar store

## LES LOCALISATEURS

### Répondre aux questions "Where? When?"

**Le sais-tu ?**

- Les mots qui servent à indiquer l'**endroit** ou le **moment** s'appellent des **localisateurs** : *IN France, IN May.*
- **Localiser** signifie "**situer quelque part** dans l'**espace** ou dans le **temps**".
- Pour localiser, on utilise des **prépositions** (*in, at, to,* etc.) suivies d'un **nom** (*in London, at the drama club* ...), ou d'**adverbes** comme *here, there, upstairs, downstairs* [lieu] et *now, then, yesterday, tomorrow* [temps].
- Les **prépositions** "accompagnent" un groupe nominal. Les **adverbes** se débrouillent tout seuls !
  *She is in the house.* [préposition] *She is inside.* [adverbe] *She is leaving tomorrow.* [adverbe]

| | | | |
|---|---|---|---|
| *IN* | | l'endroit est comme une boîte | I'm in my house, in London. |
| *AT* | ●X | l'endroit est comme un point sur une carte ou un cadran | Meet me at 8 o'clock, at the drama club! |
| *TO* | → X | on se dirige vers (destination) | I'm going to England. It's five to seven. |
| *PAST* | | on a dépassé un point de repère | Go past the supermarket. It's five past seven. |
| *FROM* | X → | on vient de (point de départ, origine) | Ben is from San Francisco. |
| *UP* | ↗ | on monte, ça augmente | Go upstairs. Prices *(les prix)* are going up. |
| *DOWN* | ↘ | on descend, ça diminue | Come downstairs. Prices are going down. |
| *NEAR* | | on est près de... ('à proximité', 'pas loin de ') | I live near New York. |
| *NEXT TO* | | on est près de... = 'juste à côté' | Romeo is sitting next to Juliet. |
| *OPPOSITE* | | on est en face de... | Romeo is sitting opposite Juliet. |
| *BETWEEN* | X●X | on est entre... et... | Julie is sitting between her parents. |
| *BEHIND* | | on est derrière | The sun is behind the clouds. |
| *IN FRONT OF* | | on est devant | Rob is sitting in front of Julie. |
| *AGAINST* | | on est contre | The desk is against the wall. |

# Grammar store

## LES VERBES IRRÉGULIERS

| *base verbale* | *prétérit* | *participe passé* | | *base verbale* | *prétérit* | *participe passé* | |
|---|---|---|---|---|---|---|---|
| be | was | been | *être* | leave | left | left | *partir, quitter* |
| beat | beat | beaten | *battre* | light | lit | lit | *allumer* |
| become | became | become | *devenir* | lose [uː] | lost [ɒ] | lost [ɒ] | *perdre* |
| begin | began | begun | *commencer* | make | made | made | *faire* |
| break | broke | broken | *casser* | meet | met | met | *rencontrer* |
| build | built | built | *construire* | pay | paid | paid | *payer* |
| buy | bought | bought | *acheter* | put | put | put | *mettre* |
| choose | chose | chosen | *choisir* | read [iː] | read [e] | read [e] | *lire* |
| come | came | come | *venir* | ride | rode | ridden | *faire du vélo** |
| cost | cost | cost | *coûter* | run | ran | run | *courir* |
| cut | cut | cut | *couper* | say | said | said | *dire* |
| do | did | done | *faire* | see | saw | seen | *voir* |
| draw | drew | drawn | *dessiner* | sell | sold | sold | *vendre* |
| dream | dreamt | dreamt | *rêver* | shoot | shot | shot | *tirer (fusil)* |
| drink | drank | drunk | *boire* | show | showed | shown | *montrer* |
| drive | drove | driven | *conduire* | sing | sang | sung | *chanter* |
| eat | ate | eaten | *manger* | sit | sat | sat | *s'asseoir* |
| feel | felt | felt | *(res)sentir* | sleep | slept | slept | *dormir* |
| fight | fought | fought | *combattre, se battre* | speak | spoke | spoken | *parler* |
| find | found | found | *trouver* | spell | spelt | spelt | *épeler* |
| forget | forgot | forgotten | *oublier* | spend | spent | spent | *dépenser* |
| get | got | got | *obtenir* | stand | stood | stood | *se tenir debout* |
| give | gave | given | *donner* | steal | stole | stolen | *voler* |
| go | went | gone | *aller* | sweep | swept | swept | *balayer* |
| grow | grew | grown | *pousser, grandir* | swim | swam | swum | *nager* |
| hang | hung | hung | *accrocher* | take | took | taken | *prendre* |
| have | had | had | *avoir* | teach | taught | taught | *enseigner* |
| hear [ɪə] | heard [ɜː] | heard [ɜː] | *entendre* | tell | told | told | *dire, raconter* |
| hold | held | held | *tenir* | think | thought | thought | *penser* |
| keep | kept | kept | *garder* | understand | understood | understood | *comprendre* |
| know | knew | known | *connaître, savoir* | wear | wore | worn | *porter* |
| lay | laid | laid | *mettre (la table)* | write | wrote | written | *écrire* |
| learn | learnt | learnt | *apprendre* | | | | |

* *ou du cheval*

# Exercise bank – Prologue

## "Be" – Les pronoms personnels sujets

**1 Complète par une forme de *be*. Dis la vérité.**
1 My name … Pierre. What ... your name?
2 I … French. What ... your nationality?
3 Jane Birkin … American. ... she English?
4 … your parents English? No, they ...
5 I … in 5e. What form ... you in?

**2 Remplace les mots soulignés par des pronoms.**
1 My English teacher speaks English.
2 Harrison Ford is a famous actor.
3 My friend and I live in the same city.
4 My school friends are friendly.
5 My Dad's car is not a Rolls Royce.

## Les "tags" avec "be"

Quand tu ajoutes un *tag* à une affirmation, c'est pour encourager le dialogue !
- Tu n'es pas sûr(e) de ce que tu affirmes et tu poses une vraie question. L'intonation à la fin du *tag* est montante ↗.
- Tu veux seulement confirmer ce dont tu es certain(e). L'intonation est alors descendante ↘.

**3 Ajoute un *tag* pour transformer ces affirmations en questions. Puis lis à haute voix (↗ sur le *tag*).**
1 You are French, …?
2 Your sister is 16, …?
3 You are not from Paris, …?
4 Your father is tall, …?
5 The Masons' children are not here, …?

**4 Transforme ces phrases en questions simples.**
Ex : He is English, isn't he? → *Is he really English?*
1 They are from New York, aren't they?
2 You are working, aren't you?
3 Paul is not an artist, is he?
4 Sue is a teacher, isn't she?
5 We are good friends, aren't we?

## Les questions en "Wh-"

**5 Complète par *who* ou par *where*. Lis la réponse avant de choisir.**
1 "... is your teacher?" "Mr Bell."
2 "... is he from?" "He is from London."
3 "... is his house?" "In Queen's Terrace."
4 "... do you live?" "In Britanny."
5 "... do you live with?" "With my mother."

**6 Pose la question et réponds.**
**Tu veux savoir ...**
1 qui est cet homme.
2 d'où il vient.
3 comment il s'appelle.
4 quel âge il a.
5 s'il est américain.

## NEED MORE PRACTICE?

**7 a. Écris ces nombres en chiffres.**
1 Five hundred and sixty seven.
2 One thousand eight hundred and one.
3 Three thousand four hundred and thirty four.
4 Six thousand and five.
5 One hundred and eleven.

**b. Écris ces nombres en lettres.**
44 - 156 - 832 - 615 - 1712

**8 Imagine ce qu'ils disent.**

# Exercise bank – Act 1

## Setting the scene — Les affaires d'école

**9 Retrouve les objets dont les mots ont été mélangés.**

pencil glue case note correction set brush stick fluid
exercise paint sharpener maths pad **book** box

## Scenes 1-2 — "Have got" et le génitif

**10 Écris deux phrases par dessin.**

*Ex:*

*Mark has got a small red car.*
*This is Mark's car.*

**11 Invente des mini-dialogues en utilisant *who* ou *whose*.**

*Ex:*

*Whose book is it? Is it Rob's?*
*Yes, it's his book, isn't it?*

## Scenes 3-4 — Les pronoms personnels sujets et compléments

| | | | | | | | | |
|---|---|---|---|---|---|---|---|---|
| sujet : | I, | you, | he, | she, | it, | we, | you, | they |
| complément : | me, | you, | him, | her, | it, | us, | you, | them |

**12 Remplace les noms soulignés par des pronoms.**

**1** James is acting. Listen to James!
**2** Sophie likes James.
**3** Rob and Kevin both like Sophie.
**4** Aliette likes James and Kevin.
**5** My friend and I love chocolate.

**13 Remplace les pronoms par des noms.**

**1** He is listening to her.
**2** She is looking at him.
**3** They are playing cards with them.
**4** We are waiting for him.
**5** They often cross it to go to the dining hall.

### Le présent simple – Le présent en "be + -ing"

**14 Construis ces phrases. Conjugue les verbes et ajoute les mots qui manquent.**

**1** Sophie / be / Irish / so / she / like / Ireland
**2** She / not / live / Dublin. She / live / London
**3** the Macguires / go / Dublin / every year
**4** Mr Macguire / drive / bus. He / be / bus driver
**5** He / work / London Transport

**15 C'est en ce moment que ça se passe. Construis des phrases concernant Sophie.**

**1** Sophie / play / with / sister. Look!
**2** What / ? / brother / do
**3** He / work / and / listen / radio / the same time.
**4** What / he / ? / listen / to
**5** He / listen / to / a musical. He / love / musicals.

# Exercise bank – Act 1

**16** **Dis ce qu'ils font. Comment réagissent-ils ? Explique ou commente.**

## NEED MORE PRACTICE?

**17** ***Be* ou *have* ? Écris six phrases sur ce personnage.**

**18** **Complète par des mots interrogatifs, puis trouve une réponse logique.**

**1** ... is that tall man?
**2** ... are these children?
**3** ... subjects do you like at school?
**4** ... highlighter is this?
**5** ... teachers have you got?

**19** **De quel jour s'agit-il ?**

**1** It is the first day of the week in England.
**2** It is the day named after the moon.
**3** It is your fifth day at school.
**4** It is the first day of the weekend.
**5** It is the day between Wednesday and Friday.

**20** **Voici où ils sont. Demande ce qu'ils font.**

Ex: Rob is in the art room. → *Is he drawing?*

**1** Sophie is in the playground.
**2** Kevin is in the music room.
**3** The children are in the dining hall.
**4** The teachers are in the staff room.
**5** The Head is in the assembly hall.

## REVISION

**21** **Classe ces mots en cinq séries. Le titre de chaque série se trouve parmi eux.**

father ruler shy Spanish mother
aunt **months** clumsy
April school things crayon Italian
family
good-tempered May
son Hindi rubber
handy sociable
daughter
German August
children
uncle July pencil case
quiet
good and bad sides languages

**22** **React.**

# Exercise bank – Act 2

## Setting the scene — Le sport

**23 Trouve trois sports et les mots qui s'y rapportent.**

### "Can / can't"

**24 Sais-tu le faire ? Pas du tout ? Un peu ? Bien ?**

**25 Ajoute le *tag*, puis réponds.**

**1** Your father can swim, ...?
**2** You can ride a bike, ...?
**3** Your mother can't sing very well, ...?
**4** Your English teacher can speak Hindi, ...?
**5** You can't play the piano, ...?

## Scenes 1-2 — L'expression des goûts avec base verbale + "-ing"

**26 Complète par le mot évoqué, puis réponds.**

**1** Do you enjoy  ?
**2** Does your friend like  ?
**3** Do you like or hate  ?
**4** Which do you prefer?  or  ?
**5**  is fun, isn't it?

**27 Complète à l'aide de *ride(s)* ou *riding*.**

**1** ... is fantastic, isn't it?
**2** How well can your parents ...?
**3** How often do they ...?
**4** My little sister loves ... too.
**5** Look! She is ... Toffee, her favourite horse.
**6** She always ... Toffee.
**7** Does she sometimes ... another horse?

### Le présent simple et la fréquence

**28 Dis avec quelle fréquence tu fais ces actions.**

**1** help your mother
**2** hoover your room
**3** phone your best friend
**4** clean your shoes
**5** watch the news on TV

**29 Pose la question avec *how often?* Puis réponds en donnant des précisions sur la fréquence.**

**1** I brush my teeth ... a day.
**2** My father goes shopping ... a week.
**3** The teacher says "Repeat, please!"
**4** Kevin helps at his father's garage.
**5** Ian walks Juliet in his wheelchair.

**30 Complète par un *tag* et réponds.**

**1** You get up early, ...?
**2** Kevin feels full of energy in the morning, ...?
**3** Before the geography lesson, he doesn't feel well, ...?
**4** He enjoys buying football badges, ...?
**5** When he is acting, he is happy, ...?

**31 Réponds en donnant des détails.**

**1** What makes you feel happy?
**2** When are you full of energy?
**3** When are you bored?
**4** What makes you jealous?
**5** At what times of day do you feel tired?

# Exercise bank – Act 2

## Scenes 3-4 — Le prétérit

**32 Classe ces marqueurs de temps en trois catégories : présent en cours, passé, fréquence.**

always, three years ago, now, rarely, in 1990, never, five minutes ago, at the moment, often, last year, sometimes, yesterday, usually, this year, last month, three days ago

**33 Donne deux renseignements par personnage.**

*Ex:* Charlie Chaplin. → *He acted in "Modern Times".*

**1** Beethoven
**2** The Lumière brothers
**3** Leonardo Da Vinci
**4** Christopher Colombus
**5** Victor Hugo

**34 Dis ce que tu sais, puis pose trois questions.**

Julius Caesar

**35 Complète par un *tag* et réponds.**

**1** Shakespeare lived a long time ago, ...?
**2** He wrote poems, ...?
**3** He didn't have any children, ...?
**4** He didn't live in Paris, ...?
**5** He was very famous, ...?

**36 Retrouve les phrases.**

**1** Jim / When / did / arrest / they / ?
**2** enjoy / the / you / Did / play / ?
**3** He / go / didn't / jogging / , / he / did / ?
**4** in / forty / November / was / Rob / 's / Mum
**5** to / reigned / 1837 / Who / from / 1901 / ?

## NEED MORE PRACTICE?

**37 Complète par *was* ou *were*.**

**1** ... your sister at home last night? Yes, she ...
**2** ... you with her? No, I ...n't.
**3** I ... at the cinema.
**4** ... the film good?
**5** The story ... boring but the actors ... brilliant.

**38 Complète pour corriger ce qui est dit.**

Ex: He didn't go to London. → *He went to Paris.*

**1** I didn't see *"Star Wars"* yesterday. I ...
**2** I got a watch for Christmas. I ...
**3** Shakespeare didn't write *"Tintin"*. He ...
**4** Dad didn't take me to the zoo. He ...
**5** I bought a crash helmet yesterday. It ...

## REVISION

**39 Dis que ...**

**1** tu sais très bien faire du cheval.
**2** tu aimes beaucoup t'occuper d'animaux.
**3** ta meilleure amie a acheté des gants hier.
**4** Beethoven était sourd quand il mourut.
**5** Ben a vu son acteur préféré sur la plage.

**40 Sais-tu demander à un ami ...**

**1** s'il est bricoleur et s'il sait réparer son vélo.
**2** s'il s'occupe souvent de son chien.
**3** quand il est né et où.
**4** ce qu'il a acheté pour l'anniversaire de son père.
**5** si sa grand-mère était française.

**41 Trouve au moins cinq actions que tu fais dans chacun de ces lieux.**

1

2

3

# Exercise bank – Act 3

## Setting the scene La nourriture – Articles – "Some, any"

**42 Change les mots en italique.**
**1** You make vinaigrette with *ice cream*.
**2** Good apples are *salty* and *greasy*.
**3** You eat mayonnaise with *chocolate*.
**4** *Junk food* is good for you.
**5** I eat *tartar steak* for breakfast.

**43 Trouve l'aliment qui se cache.**
**1** The Chinese eat tons of it.
**2** You put it in tea or coffee if you have a sweet tooth.
**3** They are small and red and grow on trees.
**4** It contains a lot of animal fat. Margarine is healthier.
**5** I love it but I can't bear Camembert.

**44 Complète par *some* ou *any*.**
**1** ... more dessert, Rob? Yes, please!
**2** Are there ... strawberries in the fruit salad?
**3** I don't want ... chocolate, thank you!
**4** There is ... jam in the cupboard, isn't there?
**5** Sorry, I can't see ...

**45 Complète par *the* ou *a(n)* si nécessaire.**
**1** Can I have ... orange juice, please?
**2** Pass me ... butter, will you?
**3** ... butter is bad for you.
**4** ... beans are in the fridge. Can you take them out?
**5** Do you prefer ... rice or ... spaghetti?

## Scenes 1-2 "Have to / had to"

**46 Complète par *have to* à la forme et au temps qui conviennent.**
**1** A scout ... be obedient and disciplined.
**2** French school children ... wear uniforms.
**3** Ian ... walk Juliet in his wheelchair.
**4** The Romans ... build a wall to stop the Picts.
**5** When he was 4, Iqbal ... work as a slave.

**47 Choisis entre *have* et *had*, puis coche les phrases qui expriment une obligation.**
**1** I always ... bad marks in French.
**2** Yesterday I ... to revise for our next French test.
**3** I ... an aunt who is a French teacher.
**4** Every Saturday I ... to do dictations with her!
**5** Last time, I ... to recite grammar rules as well.

**48 Complète par *have* ou *do* à la forme et au temps qui conviennent, puis réponds en disant la vérité.**
**1** ... your best friend got a mountain bike?
**2** ... you have to help him / her repair it?
**3** ... your mother have to drive you to school?
**4** ... she have to drive you yesterday?
**5** ... you finished your exercise now?

**49 Ajoute un *tag* et réponds.**
**1** Scouts have to learn how to make fires, ...?
**2** A Girl Guide has to be a DIY person, ...?
**3** You don't have to cook to get the Collector's Badge, ...?
**4** You like crunchy apples, ...?
**5** You don't often eat sweet and sour pork, ...?

**50 Dis la vérité en ajoutant un adverbe de fréquence : *always, usually, never,* etc.**
**1** My mother has to do the cooking.
**2** I have to clear the table.
**3** My friend has to help me with my maths.
**4** I enjoy doing my maths exercises.
**5** My English teacher gets angry.

**51 Dis ce qu'il faut faire pour obtenir ce badge.**
*To get this badge, you ...*

# Exercise bank – Act 3

## Scenes 3-4 Trop ou pas assez ? – Auxiliaires modaux

**52** **Quel est le problème ? Dis-le : *He / She can't ... because ...***

**53** **Recopie la première partie des phrases. Retrouve ensuite la subordonnée et recopie-la en la complétant.**

**1** They didn't manage to fly their kite *(cerf-volant)*
**2** They had to take the bus
**3** They couldn't go for the picnic
**4** They couldn't park outside the supermarket
**5** They shouldn't take that mountain road

**a** because they were too tired to ...
**b** because there were too many ...
**c** because it is too risky, they might have an ...
**d** because there was not enough ...
**e** because it rained and it wasn't ... enough.

**54** **Dis ce qu'ils devraient ou ne devraient pas faire.**

## NEED MORE PRACTICE?

**55** **Ajoute un *tag* et réponds par oui.**

**1** I must turn right here, ...?
**2** In England, you have to drive on the left,...?
**3** You must stop at pedestrian crossings, ...?
**4** You mustn't exceed 30 mph in a town, ...?
**5** You can take your driving test at 17, ...?

**56** **Termine ces phrases à l'aide de *enough* ou de *too*.**

**1** Sophie couldn't sunbathe because ...
**2** She wanted to make a strawberry tart, but there ...
**3** She shouldn't talk so long on the mobile because ...
**4** She mustn't use her skateboard on the road. It is ...
**5** Mr Macguire must drive more slowly. He goes ...

## REVISION

**57** **Choisis l'auxiliaire modal qui convient.**

**1** That child ... be more polite to his mother.
**2** ... I ask you a favour? Yes, you ...
**3** You ... be late again tomorrow!
**4** He is too fat. He ... eat so much junk food.
**5** When I was three, I ... speak English.

**58** **Comment dirais-tu ... ?**

**1** que trop de gens conduisent trop vite.
**2** qu'ils devraient être plus prudents.
**3** que vous ne devez pas doubler à un carrefour.
**4** que vous devez regarder à droite avant de traverser.
**5** que personne ne devrait oublier le code de la route.

# Exercise bank – Act 4

## Setting the scene

## La maison – "Going to"

**59 Trouve l'objet décrit.**

**1** It is something you put your glasses on before you go to sleep.
**2** You can put books or clothes in it. It is often messy.
**3** It is usually comfortable and you sit in it.
**4** You put them on the walls to decorate your room.
**5** It is something useful if you want to wake up on time.

**60 Écris une devinette par objet.**

**61 Que font-ils en ce moment ? Que vont-ils faire ?**

## Scenes 1-2

## L'expression du futur

**62 Complète par *will / won't, may* ou *might*.**

**1** Sophie is ill. She ... be absent for the English test tomorrow. *(pas très sûr)*
**2** Don't worry! I'm sure she ... be better. *(sûr que oui)*
**3** In May, she ... have to go to Dublin. *(pas sûr du tout)*
**4** So she ... be in London in May. *(sûr que non)*
**5** But she ... be back for James's party in June. *(sûr que oui)*

**63 Réponds en donnant des précisions.**

**1** Will you speak English tomorrow?
**2** You won't be on holiday next week, will you?
**3** How will you feel on June 30th?
**4** Do you think you will go to university?
**5** Where will you live when you are an adult?
**6** Will you be 25 in 2025?

**64 Termine ces phrases. Présent ou futur ?**

**1** My parents will buy me a new bike if ...
**2** I will be pleased if ...
**3** My mother will be upset if ...
**4** I will take my driving test when ...
**5** I'll tell you about it when ...
**6** When ..., I ...

**65 Demande-moi ...**

**1** à quelle heure ma fête d'anniversaire débutera.
**2** qui j'ai l'intention d'inviter.
**3** combien de personnes viendront.
**4** ce que je vais porter.
**5** si tu peux aider lorsque la fête sera terminée.
**6** quel âge j'aurai exactement.

# Exercise bank – Act 4

## Scenes 3-4 "Will have to – Will be able to" – Suggestions

**66** **Recopie la première partie des phrases. Retrouve ensuite la subordonnée et recopie-la en la complétant.**

**1** Ian will have to go to university
**2** Ben won't be able to have a shed
**3** James won't have to walk to school
**4** Mark will have to promise he'll stop smoking
**5** Rob will be able to surf the net

**a** if he wants to become ...
**b** when his father ... him a computer.
**c** when he gets ...
**d** if nobody ... him.
**e** if he ...

**67** **Quelle sera la conséquence ? Utilise *will / won't have to* ou *will / won't be able to.***

**1** Ben wants to go for a walk, but it is raining, so ...
**2** He can't find his tennis racket, so ...
**3** Sharon's new school is quite near, so ...
**4** The fridge is nearly empty, so ...
**5** Sophie has lost her workbook, so ...

**68** **Voici des réponses. Retrouve les suggestions qui ont été faites. Varie les formules.**

**1** Sorry, I haven't got my crash helmet.
**2** Good idea, but I don't know where my tent is.
**3** Yes, let's. But I'd like to see Versailles this time.
**4** Why not? I love thrillers.
**5** No, it's sunny. Let's go to the beach instead.

## NEED MORE PRACTICE?

**69** **Devine la suite ! Utilise *be going to.***

**1** It is cloudy. I am sure ...
**2** Sophie is buying flour, eggs and sugar. I think ...
**3** The boys are playing ball in the living room. They ...
**4** Mark wants to marry his girlfriend, so ...
**5** Mrs Adams is carrying the old cushions. Perhaps ...

**70** **James choisit un cadeau pour Ian. Dis ce qu'il achètera sûrement, peut-être, certainement pas. Pourquoi ?**

**71** **Retrouve les phrases complètes. Souligne la proposition principale.**

**1** Life will be different for them
**2** If Sophie paints her room blue,
**3** He'll buy her a big bunch of roses
**4** Sue might agree to marry Mark
**5** If it is sunny enough

**a** next time she invites him to dinner.
**b** I may go hiking.
**c** when he stops smoking.
**d** when they have a baby.
**e** she will have to change her rug and her curtains.

## REVISION

**72** **Complète.**

**1** Shall we go windsurfing if ...
**2** Mark may give Sue his car when ...
**3** If Aliette wants to be a vet, ...
**4** After some riding lessons, Kevin ...
**5** If it rains this afternoon, Ben ...
**6** Mark will go to the party if ...

**73** **Comment dirais-tu que ... ?**

**1** s'il pleut, tu as l'intention de ranger ta chambre.
**2** si la cousine de Ian peut venir, elle se déguisera en reine.
**3** il se pourrait que Sue épouse Mark l'an prochain.
**4** les amis de Ben pourront voir les plus grands arbres du monde quand ils visiteront le parc national.
**5** Sophie devra faire plus attention la prochaine fois qu'elle fera des crêpes.

## Setting the scene La description physique - Les comparatifs

**74 Classe les mots en trois catégories :**
***your face - your body - physical characteristics***

arm tall eyes hand leg strong ears foot fat nose hair plump neck slim mouth lips gigantic shoulders knees fingers healthy toes

**75 Dessine le portrait de cet homme.**
Mr Mo is very fat. His hair is grey, medium long and straight. His eyes are small and green. His nose is very long and his ears are enormous. He has only got one tooth which is black and he wears glasses. He has got a lot of freckles and he even has a beauty spot near his right eye. He really has an awful face!

**76 Complète par *(not) as ... as*, puis ajoute le *tag*.**
**1** Ian is ... athletic ... his friends, ...?
**2** Romeo is ... clever ... Juliet, ...?
**3** Aliette's aunt is ... young ... her husband, ...?
**4** Sophie's hair is ... red ... her sister's, ...?
**5** Kirk Douglas was ... attractive ... his son, ...?

**77 Compare ...**
**1** la corpulence de deux membres de ta famille.
**2** la taille de deux camarades.
**3** ta force et celle d'un membre de ta famille.
**4** l'élégance de deux de tes professeurs.
**5** les talents artistiques de deux de tes camarades.

## Scenes 1-2 Le superlatif - Les grands nombres

**78 Chacun, dans ce club de gym, bat un record. Lequel ?**

**79 a. Écris ces nombres en lettres.**
1,345 346,009 1,234,444

**b. Écris ces nombres en chiffres.**
**1** One thousand three hundred and twenty two.
**2** Two hundred thousand three hundred and one.
**3** One million three hundred thousand and fifteen.

**80 Complète par un adjectif, puis réponds.**
**1** How ... is the Eiffel Tower? 250 metres?
**2** How ... is your grandmother? 90?
**3** How ... is Hadrian's wall? 10 kilometres?
**4** How ... can the TGV go? 200 km an hour?
**5** How ... is Rhode Island? As big as France?

**81 Dis-le en anglais !**
**1** Compare deux animaux que tu connais bien.
**2** Parle des records d'un champion olympique.
**3** Parle d'un record dans ta famille.
**4** Dis quel record tu bats dans ta classe.
**5** Décris ton meilleur ami.

**82 Trouve la question.**
**1** France? It is 551,602 sq.km.
**2** Hadrian's Wall? It is nearly 2,000 years old.
**3** It is 4,807 metres high.
**4** I can swim 100 metres in 1'10".
**5** My hand? It is 15 cm long.

## Scenes 3-4

### "Present perfect" - "Ago"

**83 Complète par *have* ou *has* et réponds.**
1 ... you forgotten the name of the capital of Italy?
2 ... your father ever been there?
3 Mark ... already lived in Italy, ... he?
4 He ... never lived in Sicily, ... he?
5 ... you ever visited Rome?

**84 Pose la question avec *have ... ever?* Réponds.**
1 English teacher / seen the Queen
2 Madonna / been to Great Britain
3 You / been abroad
4 You / bought your teacher a present
5 French teacher / read a book by Balzac

**85 Fabrique les phrases pour parler des expériences de ces personnes.**
1 my grandmother / never / take / the TGV
2 I / already / eat / couscous
3 you / ever / drink / Greek wine / ?
4 my rich aunt / already / buy / a bag from Dior
5 the Head / ever / speak / to your parents / ?

**86 Complète par *ever* ou *already*.**
1 My mother has ... been to London.
2 Have you ... been there?
3 I have ... read that book.
4 Has your father ... lived abroad?
5 I've ... eaten Chinese food. I like it.

**87 Mesure le temps écoulé en utilisant *ago*.**
1 I saw him last September.
2 I went to England in 1999.
3 She bought her jeans last Tuesday.
4 This church was built in 1270.
5 I heard him on the radio at ten o'clock.

**88 Réponds avec *ago*. Dis la vérité.**
1 When did you start learning English?
2 When was your last birthday?
3 When did you last take a train?
4 When did you last see the President on TV?
5 When did you last go to the cinema?

## NEED MORE PRACTICE?

**89 Voici la chambre de Kevin. Réagis !**
*Ex: He has already ... . When did he (last) ...?*

## REVISION

**90 Comment dirais-tu ...**
1 que tu ressembles à ton arrière grand-mère.
2 que ta tante est aussi amusante que ton oncle.
3 qu'ils sont déjà allés à Chicago.
4 qu'ils y sont allés il y a trois ans.
5 qu'ils ont vu le plus haut gratte-ciel des USA.

**91 Demande-moi ...**
1 si je suis déjà allé en Australie.
2 si la Californie est plus peuplée que le Texas.
3 si l'Alaska est le plus grand état des États-Unis.
4 si j'ai déjà mangé du haggis en Ecosse.
5 quel est le plus beau pays que j'aie jamais visité.

# Exercise bank - Epilogue

## La ville

**92 Où Mark est-il allé hier ?**
**1** First he started the day with a haircut.
**2** Then he bought a very precious old Chinese vase.
**3** After that he had hot curry for lunch.
**4** In the afternoon he bought a clown's costume.
**5** Finally he bought some bread and some steak.

**93 Qu'achète-t-on dans ces lieux ? Complète.**
**1** At the baker's, you buy ... (3 things)
**2** At the butcher's, you buy ... (5 things)
**3** At the chemist's, ... (3 things)
**4** At the grocer's, ... (5 things)
**5** At the clothes shop, ... (5 things)

## "Be + -ing" au présent et au prétérit

**94 Complète par *be* au présent ou au prétérit.**
**Meg:** Look at this photo of John's birthday! We ... all enjoying ourselves, aren't we?
**Pat:** John ... not on the photo. What ... he doing?
**Meg:** We gave him a trumpet. He ... playing it in the garden. And listen! He ... playing it again now.

**95 Complète par le prétérit en *be* + *-ing.***
**A:** What ... you (do) yesterday at 4pm?
**B:** At four, I ... (walk) my dog in the park.
It ... (rain) and the wind ... (blow) hard.
Lots of children ... (fly) their kites.
**A:** Well, I ... (read) the London Gazette at home. And I ... (listen) to a CD at the same time.

**96 Que se passait-il sur la péniche des Smiths à 11 heures hier ?**

## Les pronoms réfléchis

**97 Complète par le pronom réfléchi qui convient.**
**1** You are very dirty! Look at ...!
**2** Did Kevin make his mask ...?
**3** We really enjoyed ... at the party.
**4** Sophie went to the dentist's by ...
**5** The Adams fixed the shed ...
**6** Ben made the cushion ...

**98 Réfléchi ou non ? Traduis.**
**1** T'es-tu bien amusé?
**2** As-tu fait ton costume toi-même ?
**3** Je me lave toujours avant le petit déjeuner.
**4** Elle est en train de se regarder dans la glace !
**5** Quand ma mère est entrée, je me regardais dans la glace du salon.

## REVISION

**99 Ajoute le *tag*, puis donne une réponse logique.**
**1** Jim Ricotti went onto the boys' boat, ...?
**2** He was dressed up as a clown, ...?
**3** The police weren't waiting for him, ...?
**4** Jim tried to escape, ...?
**5** But the police managed to arrest him, ...?

**100 *Be* + *-ing* ou prétérit simple ? Choisis.**
Yesterday, I *(went / was going)* to the dry cleaner's, when I *(met / was meeting)* a friend outside the baker's. She *(went / was going)* to the hairdresser's but we *(decided / were deciding)* to have a cup of coffee. We *(enjoyed / were enjoying)* ourselves enormously when we *(heard / were hearing)* screams.

# Word shop

- Abréviations : aux. : auxiliaire ; pl. : pluriel ; adj. : adjectif ; v. : verbe ; prét. : prétérit ; part. : participe passé ; US : américain.
- Le lexique comprend les mots utiles pour le travail personnel.
- Les mots "transparents" comme *garage, address, tomato,* ne figurent pas dans le lexique.
- Les traductions proposées s'appliquent aux mots dans le contexte qui est le leur dans ce manuel.

## A

**able to (be)** (v.) être capable de
**about** à propos de, environ
**above** ci-dessus, au-dessus
**abroad** à l'étranger
**accommodation** logement
**across** à travers
**act** (v.) jouer (théâtre)
**add** (v.) ajouter
**ads** petites annonces / pub
**advice** conseil
**after** après
**afternoon** après-midi
**again** encore
**against** contre
**ago** il y a (temps)
**agree** (v.) être d'accord
**ahead** devant, tout droit
**alive** vivant
**all** tout, tous, toutes
**all right** d'accord, pas mal
**allowed** permis
**alone** seul(e)
**aloud** à haute voix
**already** déjà
**also** aussi, également
**always** toujours
**a.m. (ante meridiem)** avant midi
**amusing** amusant(e)
**and** et
**angry** fâché(e), en colère
**another** un(e) autre
**answer** (v.) répondre
**any** du, de la, des
**anybody** quelqu'un, n'importe qui
**not anything** rien
**anyway** de toute façon
**anyone** personne, quelqu'un
**apple** pomme
**apple pie** tourte aux pommes
**area** endroit, région
**arm** bras
**armchair** fauteuil
**around** autour de, vers
**arrest** (v.) arrêter
**arrival** arrivée
**as** que, comme
**as ... as** aussi ... que
**ask** (v.) demander
**at** à
**ate** prét. de **eat**
**Atishoo!** Atchoum!
**attend** (v.) assister
**attic** grenier
**attractive** attirant
**aunt, auntie** tante, tatie
**autumn** automne
**avoid** (v.) éviter
**aware** au courant
**away** loin, au loin
**awful(ly)** terrible(ment)

## B

**back** dos, arrière, idée de retour
**bacon** lard fumé
**bad** mauvais, mal
**badge** médaille, insigne
**bag** sac
**bake** (v.) cuire au four
**baker** boulanger
**bakery** boulangerie-pâtisserie
**ballpen** stylo à bille
**basket** panier, corbeille
**bath** bain
**bathroom** salle de bains
**batter** pâte à crêpe
**be** (v.) être
**beach** plage
**bean** haricot
**bear** ours
**bear** (v.) supporter
**beat** (v.) battre
**beaten** battu
**beautiful** beau, belle
**became** prét. de **become**
**because** parce que
**become** (v.) devenir
**bed** lit
**bedroom** chambre
**bedside table** table de chevet
**beef** bœuf (viande)
**been** part. passé de **be**
**beer** bière
**before** avant, devant
**begin** (v.) commencer
**beginning** début
**behind** derrière
**believe** (v.) croire
**belong** (v.) **(to)** appartenir (à)
**bell** cloche, sonnerie
**below** dessous
**best (the)** (le) (la) meilleur(e)
**better** meilleur(e), mieux
**between** entre
**big** grand(e), important(e)
**bike** vélo
**bingo** loto
**bird** oiseau
**birth** naissance
**birthday** anniversaire
**bit (a)** un peu
**black** noir(e)
**blackboard** tableau noir
**blow** (v.) souffler
**blue** bleu(e)
**board** tableau (noir), planche
**boarder** pensionnaire
**boarding school** pensionnat
**boat** bateau
**book** livre
**bookshop** librairie
**boot** botte
**bored (be)** (v.) s'ennuyer
**boring** ennuyeux(-euse)
**born** né(e)
**both** tous les deux
**bottle** bouteille
**bottom (at the)** (en) bas
**bought** prét. de **buy**
**bowl** bol
**box** boîte
**boy** garçon
**brain** cerveau
**brand** marque (commerciale)
**bread** pain
**break** (v.) casser
**breakfast** petit déjeuner
**breed** race (pour un animal)
**bright** vif(-ve), clair(e), intelligent(e)
**brilliant** génial(e)
**bring** (v.) apporter
**Britain** la Grande-Bretagne
**British** Britannique
**broad** large
**broke** prét. de **break**
**broken** cassé(e)
**brother** frère
**brown** brun(e)
**Brownie** "Jeannette"
**brush** (v.) brosser
**build** (v.) construire

**building** immeuble, bâtiment
**bulb** ampoule
**bunch** bouquet
**bury** (v.) enterrer
**businessman** hommes d'affaires
**busy** occupé(e), affairé(e)
**but** mais
**butcher** boucher
**butter** beurre
**butterfly** (pl. **-ies**) papillon
**buy** (v.) acheter
**by** par, de
  **by the way** à propos
**bye** au revoir

## C

**cake** gâteau
**call** (v.) appeler, téléphoner
**called** nommé, qui s'appelle
**came** prét. de **come**
**camera** appareil photo
**can** (aux. modal) pouvoir, savoir
**candies (US)** bonbons
**cap** casquette, bonnet de bain
**capital letter** majuscule
**caption** légende (d'un dessin)
**car** voiture
**card** carte
**cardboard** carton
**careful (to be)** faire attention
**caretaker** concierge
**carpet** moquette
**carriage** voiture, wagon
**carry** (v.) porter
**cartoon** dessin animé
**cast** plâtre
**castle** château fort
**cat** chat
**catch** (v.) attraper, saisir
**cattle** bétail, vaches
**ceiling** plafond
**celebrity** personne célèbre
**century** siècle
**certainly** certainement
**chair** chaise, fauteuil
**chalk** craie
**challenge** (v.) défier
**chance** risque
**character** personnage
**chart** grille
**chat** (v.) bavarder
**cheap** bon marché
**cheat** (v.) tricher
**check** (v.) vérifier
**cheese** fromage
**chemist** pharmacien(-ne)
**chemistry** la chimie
**cherry** cerise
**chess** les échecs (jeu)
**chestnut** châtaigne, brun(e)
**chew** (v.) mâcher
**chicken** poulet
**child (pl. children)** enfant
**childhood** enfance
**chin** menton
**chips** frites
**choice** choix
**choose** (v.) choisir
**chore** corvée ménagère
**chose** prét. de **choose**
**Christmas** Noël
**church** église
**circle** cercle
**citizen** citoyen
**clean** propre
**clean** (v.) nettoyer
**clean up** (v.) tout nettoyer
**clear** clair(e), dégagé(e)
**clear** (v.) débarrasser
**clever** habile, intelligent(e)
**cloak** cape, manteau
**cloakroom** vestiaire
**clock** horloge, pendule
  **clock radio** radio-réveil
**close** près
**closed** fermé
**clothes** vêtements
**cloud(y)** nuage / nuageux (-euse)
**clue** indice
**clumsy** maladroit(e)
**coat** manteau
**cocoa** cacao
**coffee** café
**coffin** cercueil
**coin** pièce de monnaie
**cold** froid(e)
**collect** (v.) collectionner
**collector** collectionneur
**colour** (v.) colorier
**comb** (v.) peigner
**come** (v.) venir
**comics** bande dessinée
**comic strip** B.D.
**comment** (v.) commenter
**commercial** publicité
**common** (en) commun
**compass(es)** boussole, compas
**compound words** mots composés
**comprehensive school** collège
**computer** ordinateur
**connect** (v.) brancher, relier, associer
**connected** branché(e)
**considerate** attentionné(e)
**contain** (v.) contenir
**cook** cuisinier(ère)
**cook** (v.) cuire
**cooking** la cuisine
**cool!** génial !
**cool** (v.) refroidir
**copybook** cahier
**cork** bouchon
**corner** coin
**corridor** couloir
**correct** (v.) corriger
**cost** (v.) coûter
**could, couldn't** prét. de **can, can't**
**count** (v.) compter
**country** pays, campagne
**(of) course** bien sûr
**cover (to take)** s'abriter
**crack** fissure
**crash helmet** casque de protection
**crazy (about)** fou (de)
**cross** (v.) traverser
**crouch** (v.) s'accroupir
**crown** couronne
**crown** (v.) couronner
**crunchy** croustillant(e), croquant(e)
**cry** (v.) pleurer, crier
**cup** tasse
**cupboard** placard
**curly** bouclé(e)
**currency** unité monétaire
**curtain** rideau
**cushion** coussin
**custard** crème anglaise
**customer** client(e)
**customs** douane
**cut** (v.) couper
**cute** mignon
**cut out** (v.) découper
**cycle** (v.) faire du vélo

## D

**dad, daddy** papa
**daily** quotidien(-ne)
**dairy products** produits laitiers
**dark** brun(e), foncé(e), sombre
**darling** chéri(e)
**daughter** fille (≠ fils)
**day** jour
**dead** mort(e)
**deaf** sourd(e)
**dealer** marchand
**dear** cher(-ère)
  **oh dear!** mon Dieu !

**delayed** retardé(e)
**deliver** (v.) livrer
**den** antre, coin à "soi"
**depressed** déprimé(e)
**describe** (v.) décrire
**desk** bureau
**destroy** (v.) détruire
**diamond** diamant
**did** prét. de **do**
**die** (v.) mourir
**diet** régime
**difficult** difficile
**dimple** fossette
**dining room** salle à manger
**dining hall** salle à manger, réfectoire
**direction** sens, itinéraire
**dirt** saleté
**dirty** sale
**disabled** handicapé
**disappear** (v.) disparaître
**discover** (v.) découvrir
**discuss** (v.) discuter
**disgusting** dégoûtant
**dish** plat
**dishwasher** lave-vaisselle
**dislikes** ce que l'on n'aime pas
**DIY (do-it-yourself)** bricolage
**do, don't, does, doesn't** aux. présent
**do** (v.) faire
**dog** chien
**doll** poupée
**done** part. passé de **do**
**door** porte
**down** mouvement vers le bas
**downstairs** en bas, rez de chaussée
**drama** drame
**drank** prét. de **drink**
**draw** (v.) dessiner
**drawing** dessin
**dreadful** épouvantable
**dream** (v.) rêver
**dress** robe
  **get dressed** (v.) s'habiller
**dress up** (v.) se déguiser
**drill** exercice
**drink** (v.) boire
**drink** boisson
**drive** (v.) aller en voiture, conduire
**driver** chauffeur
**drop** (v.) laisser tomber
**drove** prét. de **drive**
**drunk** part. passé de **drink**
**dry** sec (sèche)
**dry cleaner's** teinturier
**duck** (v.) se baisser subitement
**due at** attendu(e) à
**during** pendant
**dust** (v.) épousseter
**duty** devoir

## E

**each** chaque, chacun(e)
**ear** oreille
**early** tôt, matinal
**earthquake** tremblement de terre
**east** l'est
**Easter** Pâques
**easy** facile
**eat** (v.) manger
**eaten** part. passé de **eat**
**egg** oeuf
**either** non plus
**elbow** coude
**elderly** âgé
**else (what)** quoi d'autre ?
**emergency** urgence, secours
**empty** vide
**empty** (v.) vider
**encore** bis
**end** fin
**enjoy** (v.) apprécier, bien s'amuser
**enough** assez
**enslave** (v.) réduire en esclavage
**eraser** (US) gomme
**escape** (v.) s'échapper
**especially** spécialement
**essential** essentiel, indispensable
**even** même
**evening** soir, soirée
**ever** déjà
**every** chaque
  **everybody** tout le monde
  **every day** tous les jours
  **everyone** tout le monde
  **everything** tout
  **everywhere** partout
**evolve** (v.) évoluer
**examine** (v.) examiner, ausculter
**exceed** (v.) dépasser
**exchange** (v.) échanger
**excited** surexcité(e), agité(e)
**exercise book** cahier
**exhausted** exténué
**exhibit** (v.) exposer
**expect** (v.) attendre
**expensive** cher(-ère)
**explain** (v.) expliquer
**eye** œil

## F

**face** visage
**face** (v.) faire face à
**fact** (un) fait
**factory** usine
**fair** blond(e), assez bien, juste
**fall** (v.) tomber
**famous** connu(e), célèbre
**fancy dress** déguisement
**far** loin
**farm(er)** ferme / fermier
**fashion** mode
**fashionable** à la mode
**fast** rapide, rapidement
**fat** gros(-se), gras(-se)
**father** père
**fatty** gras
**feed** (v.) nourrir
**feel** (v.) sentir, ressentir
**feeling** sentiment
**feet** pluriel de **foot**
**few** peu, quelque
**fight** (v.) combattre, bagarrer
**figure** silhouette, ligne
**file** dossier
**fill** (v.) remplir
**find (out)** (v.) trouver, rechercher
**fine** bien, beau
**finger** doigt
**fingerprint** empreinte digitale
**fire** feu
  **fireman** pompier
**first** premier(-ère), d'abord
  **first name** prénom
**fish** poisson
**fish** (v.) pêcher (des poissons)
**fit** en forme
**fitness** forme physique
**fix** (v.) (US) réparer
**flag** drapeau
**flat** appartement
**flew** prét. de **fly**
**flight** vol (avion)
**floor** plancher, parquet, étage
**florist** fleuriste
**flour** farine
**flower** fleur
**flown** part. passé de **fly**
**fly** (v.) (faire) voler, prendre l'avion
**foggy** brumeux(-euse)
**follow** (v.) suivre
**food** nourriture
**foot (pl. feet)** pied
**foot** unité de mesure, approx. 24.5 cm
**for** pour, pendant

**forbidden** interdit
**forget** (v.) oublier
**forget-me-not** myosotis
**forgot** prét. de **forget**
**forgotten** part. passé de **forget**
**form** classe
**fortunately** heureusement
**found** prét. & part. passé de **find**
**founder** fondateur
**fought** prét. de **fight**
**fox** renard
**freckle** tache de rousseur
**freeway** autoroute (US)
**freeze** (v.) s'immobiliser, geler
**freedom** liberté
**fridge** réfrigérateur
**friend** ami(e)
**friendly** amical(ement)
**fries** frites
**frock** robe
**from** de (origine)
**from now on** à partir de maintenant
**front (on the)** devant
**(in) front (of)** devant
**fry** (v.) frire
**full** plein(e)
**fun** amusement
**funny** drôle, amusant(e)
**funds** fonds, argent
**furniture** meubles, mobilier

## G

**game** jeu, sport
**garden** jardin
**gardener** jardinier
**gardening** jardinage
**garrison** garnison
**gate** portail
**gave** prét. de **give**
**get** (v.) acheter, aller chercher
**get along** (v.) bien s'entendre
**get dressed** (v.) s'habiller
**get in** (v.) entrer, monter
**get off** (v.) descendre
**get out of** (v.) sortir
**get ready** (v.) se préparer
**get up** (v.) se lever
**get well** (v.) se remettre
**get home** (v.) rentrer
**get married** (v.) se marier
**get rid of** (v.) se débarrasser de
**get undressed** (v.) se déshabiller
**ghost** fantôme
**girl** fille (≠ garçon)
**give** (v.) donner
**given** part. passé de **give**
**glad** content(e)
**glass(es)** verre(s), lunettes
**glove** gant
**glow** (v.) luire
**glue** colle
**go** (v.) aller, sortir, partir
**go away** (v.) s'en aller
**go past** (v.) passer devant, dépasser
**going to (be)** (v.) aller (faire)
**goldfish** poisson rouge
**gone** part. passé de **go**
**good** bon, bien
**gosh!** mince alors !
**got** prét. & part. passé de **get**
**graceful** gracieux(-euse)
**granny** mamie
**graph** graphique
**greasy** gras
**great** grand, formidable
**great-grandparent** arrière grand-parent
**greedy** gourmand(e), goinfre
**green** vert(e)
**greengrocer** marchand de légumes
**greet** (v.) saluer
**greeting** salutation
**grew** prét. de **grow**
**grey** gris(e)
**grid** grille
**grocer** épicier
**groceries** provisions
**ground** sol
**ground-floor** rez-de-chaussée
**grow** (v.) (faire) pousser
**grow up** (v.) grandir
**grown** part. passé de **grow**
**guard** (v.) surveiller
**guess** (v.) deviner
**guest** invité

## H

**had** prét. de **have**
**haggis** panse de brebis farcie
**hair** cheveux
**hairdresser** coiffeur, coiffeuse
**hairy** poilu
**half** demi(e)
**halfway** à mi-chemin
**hall** entrée, vestibule
**ham** jambon
**hand** main
**handlebars** guidon
**handy** bon bricoleur, habile
**hang** (v.) pendre, suspendre
**happen** (v.) arriver, se passer
**happy** heureux(-euse), joyeux(-euse)
**hard** dur(e)
**hat** chapeau
**hate** (v.) détester
**haunted** hanté(e)
**have (got)** (v.) avoir, posséder
**have** (v.) **(a meal)** prendre
**have to** (v.) devoir
**head** tête
**Head (headmaster)** le principal
**heading** titre
**healthy** en bonne santé
**hear** (v.) entendre
**heard** prét. & part. passé de **hear**
**heavy** lourd(e)
**height** taille, hauteur
**helmet** casque
**help** (v.) aider, servir
**her** elle, à elle
**here** ici, voici
**herself** elle-même
**Hi!** Salut!
**hid** prét. de **hide**
**hidden** part. passé de **hide**
**hide** (v.) (se) cacher
**high** haut(e)
**highlight** (v.) surligner
**highlighter** surligneur
**highway** (US) autoroute
**highway code** code de la route
**hike** (v.) faire de la marche à pied
**hill** colline
**him** lui
**himself** lui-même
**hire** (v.) louer
**his** à lui
**hit** (v.) frapper
**hobby** passe-temps
**hold** (v.) tenir
**hold up** (v.) lever
**hole** trou
**holiday(s)** vacances
**home** foyer, chez soi
**at home** à la maison
**go home** (v.) rentrer chez soi
**homework** devoirs
**honey** miel, chéri
**hoover** (v.) passer l'aspirateur
**hope** (v.) espérer
**horse** cheval
**hot** très chaud, épicé
**hour** heure
**house** maison
**household** la maisonnée

**housework** le ménage
**how** comment, comme
**How are you?** Comment ça va ?
**How many...?** Combien... ?
**How much...?** Combien... ?
**How old...?** Quel âge... ?
**How tall...?** Combien mesure... ?
**How well...?** Comment ... ?
**however** cependant
**hundred** cent
**hungry** affamé(e)
**hunter** chasseur
**hurricane** ouragan
**hurry (up)** (v.) se dépêcher
**husband** mari

## I

**ice-cream** crème glacée
**ice skate** (v.) patiner sur glace
**if** si
**ill** malade
**improve** (v.) améliorer
**in** dans, en
**in charge** responsable
**inch** pouce (mesure anglaise = 2,5 cm)
**include** (v.) inclure, comprendre
**Indian** Indien(ne)
**indeed** vraiment, en vérité
**indoors** à l'intérieur
**injured** blessé
**inside** à l'intérieur
**instead (of)** au lieu (de), à la place (de)
**instructor** moniteur
**interesting** intéressant(e)
**into** dans, en
**introduce** (v.) présenter
**investigate** enquêter
**Irish** Irlandais(e)
**iron** (v.) repasser
**it** elle, il, lui, la (pour une chose)
**IT (Information Technology)** l'informatique
**item** élément, rubrique
**its** son, sa, ses

## J

**jacket** veste
**jailed** emprisonné(e)
**jam** confiture
**jar** pot
**jersey** maillot
**jewel** bijou
**jigsaw puzzle** puzzle
**job** métier, travail
**join** (v.) joindre
**joke** blague
**juice** jus
**juicy** juteux, juteuse
**July** juillet
**jump** (v.) sauter
**junk food** nourriture industrielle

## K

**keep** (v.) garder, maintenir, ranger
**keep away** (v.) éloigner
**keep in touch** (v.) rester en contact
**keep** (v.) **+ V + ing** continuer à
**kept** prét. & part passé de **keep**
**key** clef, légende (carte)
**keyring** porte-clefs
**kick** (v.) donner un coup de pied
**kill** (v.) tuer
**kind** gentil(-le), aimable
**king** roi
**kingdom** royaume
**kitchen** cuisine
**kiss** un baiser
**kitten** chaton
**knee** genou
**knew** prét de **know**
**knife(ves)** couteau(x)
**know** (v.) savoir, connaître
**known** connu(e)
**known** part. passé de **know**

## L

**lady** dame
**land** terre
**lap (on my / your, etc.)** sur les genoux
**large** grand(e)
**last** dernier(-ère)
**late** tard, en retard
**laugh** (v.) rire
**law** loi
**lay the table** (v.) mettre la table
**layout** maquette, disposition
**lazy** paresseux(-euse)
**learn** (v.) apprendre, étudier
**least (at)** au moins
**least (the)** le moins
**leave** (v.) quitter, partir
**left** (à) gauche
**left** prét. & part. passé de **leave**
**leg** jambe
**lemon** citron
**lend** (v.) prêter
**lent** prét. & part. passé de **lend**
**less** moins
**lesson** cours
**let** (v.) laisser
**let's go** allons
**let's have fun!** amusons-nous !
**let's see!** voyons !
**library** bibliothèque
**life** vie
**light** lumière, lumineux, léger
**light** (v.) allumer
**like** comme
**like** (v.) aimer
**likes (≠ dislikes)** ce que l'on aime
**line** ligne
**lip** lèvre
**listen to** (v.) écouter
**litter** ordures
**little** petit(e)
**little (a)** (un) peu
**live** (v.) vivre, habiter
**live (aɪ)** en direct
**living room** salle de séjour
**local** du coin
**locate** (v.) situer
**locker** casier
**long** longtemps, long, longue
**look at** (v.) regarder
**look for** (v.) chercher
**look after** (v.) s'occuper de
**look like** (v.) (se) ressembler (à)
**look out!** Attention!
**loom** métier à tisser
**lose** (v.) perdre
**lost** perdu(e)
**lot (a lot of, lots of)** beaucoup
**loudspeacker** haut-parleur
**love** (v.) aimer
**lovely** beau (belle), joli(e)
**luck** chance
**luckily** heureusement, par chance
**lucky (be)** (v.) avoir de la chance
**lunch** déjeuner, repas de midi
**lyrics** paroles (d'une chanson)

## M

**mad** fou, folle
**made** fait, prét. & part. passé de **make**
**magnet** aimant
**main** principal
**make** marque
**make** (v.) faire, fabriquer
**makeup** maquillage
**man (pl. men)** homme
**manage** (v.) réussir, se débrouiller

**manner** façon, manière
**many** beaucoup de (+ pluriel)
**map** carte
**mark** note (scolaire)
**marry** (v.) épouser
**mask** masque
**match** (v.) faire correspondre
**matchbox** boîte d'allumettes
**matter (what's the matter?)** que se passe-t-il ?
**may** (aux. modal) possibilité, permission
**maybe** peut-être
**meal** repas
**mean** (v.) vouloir dire, signifier
**meant** prét. & part. passé de **mean**
**meat** viande
**medal** médaille
**medicine** médicament
**medium** moyen
**meet** (v.) rencontrer
**meeting** rendez-vous, rencontre
**men** pl. de **man**
**Merry (Christmas)** Joyeux (Noël)
**mess(y)** désordre, en désordre
**met** prét. & part. passé de **meet**
**mice** pl. de **mouse**
**middle** milieu
**midnight** minuit
**might** prét. de **may**
**mile** unité de mesure, approx. 1,6 km
**milk** lait
**milkman** laitier
**mind** (v.) se soucier de, faire attention
  **I don't mind** Celà m'est égal
  **never mind** peu importe
**mine** le(s) mien(s), la mienne, les miennes
**mint** menthe
**miserable** triste, malheureux
**mistake** faute, erreur
**model** maquette
**money** l'argent
**monkey** singe
**month** mois
**moon** lune
**more** davantage, plus
**morning** matin, matinée
**most (the)** le plus
**mother** mère
**motorway** autoroute
**motto** devise
**mountain** montagne
**mouse** souris
**mouth** bouche
**move** (v.) déménager, bouger
**movie(s)** (US) film (le cinéma)
**much** (adv.) beaucoup
  **very much** (adv.) très
  **too much** trop
**Mum, Mummy** maman
**mummy** momie
**mushroom** champignon
**musical** musicien (adj.), comédie musicale
**must** (aux. modal) devoir
**myself** moi-même

## N

**name** nom
**name** (v.) nommer, citer
**nasty** méchant
**narrow** étroit(e)
**naughty** vilain
**near** près de
**nearby** à côté de, près de
**nearly** presque
**neck** cou
**need** (v.) avoir besoin de
**neighbour** voisin(e)
**neither ... nor** ni ... ni
**nephew** neveu
**net** filet
**never** (ne) ... jamais
**new** nouveau, nouvelle, neuf(-ve)
**news** nouvelles, journal télévisé
**newsagent** marchand de journaux
**newspaper** journal
**next** prochain(e)
**nice** joli(e), gentil(le), agréable,
**nickname** surnom, petit nom
**night** nuit
**nightmare** cauchemar
**no** pas (de)
**nobody** personne
**noise** bruit
**noisy** bruyant(e)
**north** le nord
**nose** le nez
**nosy** curieux
**note down** (v.) noter
**nothing** rien
**novel** roman
**now** maintenant
**number** numéro, nombre
**nurse** infirmier, infirmière

## O

**obey** (v.) obéir
**object** objet
**odd** étrange
  **the odd one out** l'intrus
**of** de
**of course** bien sûr
**off** idée de séparation, éteint
**offer** (v.) offrir
**often** souvent
**oil** huile
**old** vieux, vieille
**on** sur, allumé(e), en marche
  **on** + date le
  **What's on?** Que joue-t-on ?
**once** une fois
**one** un, une, le, la
**only** seulement
  **only child** enfant unique
**open** ouvert(e)
**open** (v.) ouvrir
**opposite** en face de, opposé,
**or** ou
**order** ordre, commande
**order** (v.) commander
**orderly** ordonné(e)
**organic** bio
**other(s)** autre(s)
**our** notre, nos
**ours** le, la, les nôtre(s)
**ourselves** nous-mêmes
**out** idée de sortir ou d'être sorti(e)
**outdoors** au-dehors, en plein air
**outfit** costume, panoplie
**outside** devant, à l'extérieur
**oven** four
**over** au dessus, plus de, fini(e)
  **over there** là-bas
  **all over** partout
**overtake** (v.) dépasser, doubler
**own** (adj.) à soi

## P

**pad** bloc, protection
**paid** prét. & part. passé de **pay**
**paint** (v.) peindre
**paintbrush** pinceau
**painter** peintre
**painting** peinture, tableau
**pancake** crêpe
**pants** pantalon
**paper** papier, journal
**parrot** perroquet
**part** rôle
**part** (v.) se séparer
**party** réception, "boum"
**pass** (v.) **(a test)** réussir (un examen)
**past** passé

**pay** salaire
**pay** (v.) payer
**pea** petit pois
**pear** poire
**pedestrian** piéton
**peel** (v.) éplucher
**pen** stylo
**pence** pl. de **penny**
**pen-friend** correspondant(e)
**pencil** crayon
**pencil case** trousse d'écolier
**pencil-sharpener** taille-crayon
**penny** (pl. **pence**) unité de monnaie anglaise
**people** gens
**pepper** poivre
**perfect(ly)** parfait(ement)
**perhaps** peut-être
**pet** animal familier, chouchou
**pick up** (v.) ramasser
**pick out** (v.) choisir, relever
**picture** image, tableau, photo
**(to the) pictures** (au) cinéma
**picture** (v.) imaginer
**pie** tourte
**piece** morceau
**pier** jetée
**pig** cochon
**piggy bank** tirelire
**pin (split pin)** épingle, (attache parisienne)
**pink** rose (couleur)
**pitch** terrain de sport
**place** lieu, endroit
**plane** avion
**plate** assiette
**play** pièce de théâtre
**play** (v.) jouer
**playground** cour de récréation
**pleasant** agréable
**please** s'il vous plaît
**pleased** content(e)
**plenty (of)** beaucoup (de)
**plump** rondelet, dodu
**p.m. (post meridiem)** après midi
**pocket** poche
**point** (v.) montrer du doigt
**point (there's no)** ça ne sert à rien
**pointed** pointu
**policeman** policier, agent
**police officer** officier de police
**police station** commissariat
**Polish** Polonais(e)
**poll** sondage
**pool** (v.) mettre en commun
**poor** pauvre, mauvais(e)
**populated** peuplé, habité
**pork** viande de porc
**postcard** carte postale
**postman** facteur
**post office** bureau de poste
**potato** pomme de terre
**pound** livre (unité de monnaie anglaise ou unité de poids)
**practise** (v.) s'entraîner
**prefer** (v.) préférer
**present** cadeau
**pretend** (v.) faire semblant
**pretty** joli(e)
**price** prix
**print** (v.) imprimer
**probably** probablement
**promise** (v.) promettre
**properly** correctement
**property** les biens
**props** accessoires (théâtre)
**provide** (v.) fournir
**pub** café
**pull** (v.) tirer
**pupil** élève
**puppy** chiot
**purple** violet(-te)
**push** (v.) pousser
**put** (v.) mettre, poser

## Q

**quake** tremblement (de terre)
**quarrel** (v.) se disputer
**quarter** quart
**queen** reine
**queue up** (v.) faire la queue
**quick(ly)** vite, rapide(ment)
**quiet** tranquille
**quite** assez, plutôt

## R

**rabbit** lapin
**race** (v.) faire la course
**rain** la pluie
**rain** (v.) pleuvoir
**raincoat** imperméable
**rainy** pluvieux(-euse)
**rang** prét. de **ring**
**rarely** rarement
**react** (v.) réagir
**read** (v.) lire
**reading** lecture
**ready** prêt(e)
**real** réel, véritable
**really** vraiment
**record** disque
**record player** tourne-disque
**red** rouge
**red-handed** la main dans le sac
**referee** arbitre
**registration** inscription
**reign** (v.) régner
**relate** (v.) raconter
**remember** (v.) se souvenir
**removal** démenagement
**rent** loyer
**repair** (v.) réparer
**repeat** (v.) répéter
**repeatedly** à maintes reprises
**report** (v.) rendre compte, raconter
**retire** (v.) prendre sa retraite
**return** retour
**ribbon** ruban
**rice** riz
**rid** (v.) **(get rid of)** se débarrasser de
**riddle** énigme, devinette
**ride** (v.) faire du vélo, du cheval
**right** correct, juste, (à) droite
**all right** d'accord
**rights** droits
**ring** bague, manège (cheval)
**ring** (v.) sonner, téléphoner
**ring binder** classeur à anneaux
**road** route
**robber** voleur
**robbery** vol
**roller-blade** (v.) faire du patin à roulettes en ligne
**roller-skate** (v.) faire du patin à roulettes
**roof** toit
**room** pièce (de la maison)
**rough copy** brouillon
**round** rond, en rond
**roundabout** rond-point
**rub** (v.) frotter
**rubber** gomme, caoutchouc
**rude** impoli(e)
**rug** tapis
**rule** règle d'un jeu
**ruler** règle, dirigeant
**run** (v.) courir
**rung** part. passé de **ring**

## S

**sad** triste
**safe** en sécurite, sûr
**safely** prudemment
**safety** sûreté, prudence

**sail** (v.) faire de la voile, aller en bateau
**salesperson** vendeur(-euse)
**salt(y)** sel, salé(e)
**same** même, semblable
**sand** sable
**sang** prét. de **sing**
**sat** prét. de **sit**
**save** (v.) sauver, économiser
**saw** prét. de **see**
**say** (v.) dire
**scary** effrayant(e)
**school** école
**science lab** laboratoire de sciences
**scissors** ciseaux
**score** (v.) marquer (point, but)
**scream** (v.) crier
**screen** écran
**scrum** mêlée (rugby)
**sea** mer
**seaside** bord de mer
**season** saison
**secretary** secrétaire
**see** (v.) voir
  **See you!** À bientôt !
**seek** (v.) chercher
**seen** part. passé de **see**
**sell** (v.) vendre
**send** (v.) envoyer
**sent** prét. & part. passé de **send**
**sentence** phrase
**series** série
**serious** sérieux(-euse), grave
**serve** (v.) servir
**set** appareil, ensemble
  **TV set** poste de télévision
**set the scene** (v.) planter le décor
**sewage** eaux usées
**shake** (v.) secouer
  **shake hands** (v.) serrer la main
**shaken** part. passé de **shake**
**shall** (aux. modal) suggestion
**shape** forme
**sharpener** *see* **pencil**
**shave** (v.) (se) raser
**shed** abri, remise
**sheep** mouton
**sheet of paper** feuille de papier
**shelf(ves)** étagère(s)
**shell** coquillage, carapace
**shine** (v.) briller
**shiny** brillant(e)
**ship** bateau
**shirt** chemise
**shoe** chaussure
**shone** prét. & part. passé de **shine**
**shook** prét. de **shake**
**shoot** (v.) tirer, abattre
**shop** magasin
**shopkeeper** commerçant(e)
**shopping** les courses
**shopping centre** centre commercial
**short** court(e), petit(e)
**shot** prêt de shoot
**should** (aux. modal) conseil, reproche
**shoulder** épaule
**shout** (v.) crier, hurler
**shout** un cri
**show** spectacle
**show** (v.) montrer
**show off** (v.) se vanter
**shower** douche, averse
**shut** (v.) fermer
**shy** timide
**sick** malade
**side** côté
**sideways** de côté
**sightseeing** visite touristique
**sign up** (v.) s'insrire
**silent** silencieux(-euse)
**silly** bête, stupide
**sing** (v.) chanter
**singer** chanteur(-euse)
**Sir!** Monsieur !
**sister** sœur
**sit (down)** (v.) être assis, s'asseoir
**size** taille, pointure
**skate** (v.) patiner
**skill** compétence
**skilful** habile, adroit(e)
**skin** peau
**skirt** jupe
**sky** ciel
**skyscraper** gratte-ciel
**slave** esclave
**slavery** esclavage
**sleep** (v.) dormir
**slept** prét. & part. passé de **sleep**
**slice** tranche
**slice** (v.) trancher
**slim** mince
**slit** fente
**slot** fente
**slow(ly)** lent(e), lentement
**slow down** (v.) ralentir
**small** petit(e)
**smart** chic (GB) / intelligent (US)
**smell** (v.) sentir
**smelly** qui sent mauvais
**smile** sourire
**smoke** (v.) fumer
**sneeze** (v.) éternuer
**snow** (v.) neiger
**snowy** neigeux(-euse)
**so** ainsi, donc
**so** (+ adj.) si, tant, tellement
  **So long!** Au revoir ! À bientôt !
**soap** savon
**sock** chaussette
**soft** doux, mou
**sold** prêt. & part. passé de **sell**
**soldier** soldat
**solve** (v.) résoudre
**some** du, de la, des, un peu, certains, certaines
  **somebody** quelqu'un
  **someone** quelqu'un
  **something** quelque chose
  **sometimes** parfois
  **somewhere** quelque part
**son** fils
**song** chanson
**soon** bientôt, tôt
**sorrow** peine, chagrin
**sorry** désolé(e)
**so-so** comme-ci, comme-ça
**sour** aigre, acide
**south** le sud
**space** espace
**Spain** Espagne
**Spanish** espagnol
**spare** (v.) mettre de côté
**spare time** temps libre
**speak** (v.) parler
**speed** vitesse
**spell** (v.) épeler
**spend** (v.) passer, dépenser
**spent** prét. & part. passé de **spend**
**spider** araignée
**spinach** épinard
**spoke** prét. de **speak**
**spoken** part. passé de **speak**
**spoon** cuillère
**spot** tâche, lieu
  **beauty spot** grain de beauté
**spot** (v.) repérer
**spring** printemps
**sprinkle** (v.) saupoudrer
**spy** (v.) espionner, observer
**square** place, carré
**staff room** salle des professeurs
**stage** scène (théâtre)
**staircase** cage d'escalier
**stairs** escalier
**stamp** timbre
**stand up** (v.) être debout, se lever
**star** étoile

**start** (v.) débuter, démarrer
**States (The)** les États-Unis
**station** gare, poste
**stay** (v.) rester, séjourner
**steal** (v.) voler (quelque chose)
**step** (bruit de) pas
**step by step** pas à pas
**stepbrother** demi-frère
**stepsister** demi-sœur
**stick** bâton
**stick** (v.) coller
**still** encore, toujours
**stir** (v.) remuer
**stole** prét. de **steal**
**stolen** part. passé de **steal**
**stood** prét. & part. passé de **stand**
**store** magasin
**store** (v.) emmagasiner
**story** histoire
**straight** droit, rectiligne, raide
**straight away** immédiatement
**stranger** inconnu(e)
**strawberry** fraise
**street** rue
**strict** sévère
**string** ficelle
**strong** fort(e)
**struggle** (v.) lutter
**stuck** prét. & part. passé de **stick**
**study** bureau (pièce)
**study** (v.) étudier
**sturdy** costaud
**subject** matière, discipline
**sudden(ly)** soudain(-ement)
**sugar** sucre
**suggest** (v.) suggérer
**suit** un costume
**summary** résumé
**summer** été
**sums** opérations (maths)
**sun** soleil
**sunbathe** (v.) prendre des bains de soleil
**sung** part. passé de **sing**
**sunglasses** lunettes de soleil
**sunny (it's)** il y a du soleil
**supplies** provisions
**support** (v.) soutenir
**supposed to be** censé être
**sure** certain(e), sûr(e)
  **sure (make)** (v.) s'assurer
**surround** (v.) encercler
**swam** prét. de **swim**
**swap** (v.) échanger
**sweater** pull
**sweep** (v.) balayer
**sweet** doux(-ce), sucré(e), mignon(-ne)
**sweetheart** petit(e) ami(e), chéri(e)
**sweet tooth** qui aime les sucreries
**swept** prét. de **sweep**
**swim** (v.) nager
  **swimmer** nageur
  **swimming** natation
  **swimming pool** piscine
**switch off** (v.) éteindre
**switch on** (v.) allumer
**swum** part. passé de **swim**

## T

**tab** petite partie qui dépasse, patte
**tag (name tag)** badge, "cavalier"
**tail** queue (animal)
**take** (v.) prendre, emmener
**take off** (v.) enlever (un vêtement), décoller (avion)
**taken** part. passé de **take**
**talk** (v.) parler
**talkative** bavard
**tall** grand(e)
**tap dancing** faire des claquettes
**tasty** goûteux
**taught** prét. & part. passé de **teach**
**tea** thé
**teach** (v.) enseigner
**teacher** professeur
**team** équipe
**teapot** théière
**tearoom** salon de thé
**Teddy bear** ours en peluche
**teeth** pl. de **tooth**
**tell** (v.) raconter, dire
**telly** télévision
**temper** humeur
**terrible** épouvantable
**than (more... than)** plus que
**thank you (thanks)** merci
**that** celui-là, ce, cela, que, qui
**them** eux
**themselves** eux-mêmes
**their** leur, leurs
**then** ensuite, alors, donc
**there ( ≠ here)** là-bas
  **there is, there are** il y a
**these** ceux-ci, ceux-là
**thick** épais
**thief** voleur
**thin** mince
**thing** chose, affaire
**think** (v.) penser, croire
**thirsty** assoiffé
**this** ceci, celui-ci, celle-ci
**those** (pl. de **that**)
**thought** pensée
**thought** prét. & part. passé de **think**
**thousand** mille
**thriller** film à suspense
**through** à travers
**tick** (v.) cocher
**tidy** en ordre, bien rangé, ordonné(e)
**tidy** (v.) ranger
**tie** cravate
**time** moment, temps, heure, fois
  **three times** trois fois
**times** période, époque
**time-table** emploi du temps
**tired** fatigué
**title** titre
**to** à, jusqu'à
**today** aujourd'hui
**toe** orteil
**together** ensemble
**told** prét. & part. passé de **tell**
**tomorrow** demain
**tonight** ce soir
**too** aussi, trop
**took** prét. de **take**
**tooth (pl. teeth)** dent
**top (at the)** (en) haut
**topic** sujet
**tortoise** tortue
**towel** serviette
**tower** tour
**town** petite ville
**toy** jouet
**traffic** circulation
  **traffic lights** feux tricolores
**trainers** chaussures de sport
**translate** (v.) traduire
**travel** (v.) voyager
**traveller** voyageur
**tree** arbre
**tremor** secousse
**trick** ruse
**trip** voyage
**trivia game** jeux de questions
**trousers** pantalon
**true** vrai(e)
**trust** (v.) faire confiance
**try** (v.) essayer
**turn** le tour
  **(in) turn** un par un
**turn** (v.) tourner
  **turn off/on** (v.) éteindre, allumer
**twice** deux fois
**tyre** pneu

## U

**ugly** laid(e)
**umbrella** parapluie
**uncle** oncle
**uncomfortable** inconfortable
**under** sous
**underground** métro
**underpass** bretelle d'autoroute (inférieure)
**understand** (v.) comprendre
**understood** prét. & part. passé de **understand**
**underwear** sous-vêtement
**undress** (v.) (se) déshabiller
**up** idée d'aller vers le haut
**upset** contrarié(e), bouleversé(e)
**upside down** à l'envers
**upstairs** en haut, à l'étage
**us** nous
**use** (v.) utiliser
**usual** habituel(-le)
**usually** d'habitude
**utilities** services (gaz, électricité,...)

## V

**V.C.R.** magnétoscope
**vegetable** légume
**venue** lieu
**very** très
**very much** beaucoup, très
**vet** vétérinaire
**violin** violon
**VIP** Very Important Person
**voice** voix

## W

**wait (for)** (v.) attendre
**waiter** serveur, garçon de café
**wake up** (v.) se réveiller
**Wales** le Pays de Galles
**walk** marche, promenade
**walk** (v.) marcher, promener **walk-man** baladeur
**wall** mur
**wallet** portefeuille
**want** (v.) vouloir
**wanted** recherché(e)
**war** guerre
**warm** chaud(e)
**warning** avertissement, attention!
**was** prét. de **be** singulier
**wash** (v.) laver
  **wash up** (v.) faire la vaisselle
  **washing machine** lave-linge
**watch** montre
**watch** (v.) regarder
**watchman** veilleur
**water** eau
**way** chemin, manière, moyen
  **by the way** à propos
**weak** faible
**wear** (v.) porter (un vêtement)
**weather** temps, climat
**wedding** cérémonie de mariage
**week** semaine
**welcome** bienvenue
**well!** bien ! eh bien !
  **how well?** de quelle manière ?
**Welsh** Gallois(e)
**went** prét. de **go**
**were** prét. de **be** pluriel
**west** ouest
**wet** mouillé
**what** que, qui, quoi
**what about -ing?** et si on (faisait)
**wheel** roue
**wheelbarrow** brouette
**wheelchair** fauteuil roulant
**when** quand
**where** où
**which** lequel, laquelle, lesquels, lesquelles, qui, que
**while** pendant que
**white** blanc, blanche
**who** qui
**whose** à qui, dont
**why** pourquoi
**wide** large
**wife (pl. wives)** épouse
**wig** perruque
**wild** sauvage
**wildlife viewing** observation de la nature
**will** (aux. modal) futur
**win** (v.) gagner (au jeu)
**wind** vent
**windsurf** (v.) faire de la planche à voile
**window** fenêtre
**windy (it's)** il fait du vent
**wine** vin
**winner** gagnant(e)
**winter** hiver
**wish** (v.) souhaiter
**with** avec
**without** sans
**wolf** loup
**woke** prét. de **wake**
**woken** part. passé de **wake**
**woman (pl. women)** femme(s)
**won** prét. de **win**
**wonderful** merveilleux(-euse)
**won't** will not
**word** mot
**wore** prét. de **wear**
**work** (v.) travailler, fonctionner
**work out** (v.) faire de l'exercice
**world** le monde
**worn** part. passé de **wear**
**worried** inquiet(-ète)
**worry** (v.) s'inquiéter
**worst (the)** le pire
**Would you like...?** Voulez-vous ...? Aimeriez-vous ...?
**wrap** (v.) envelopper
**write** (v.) écrire
**writer** écrivain
**written** part. passé de **write**
**wrong** faux, fausse
**wrote** prét. de **write**

## Y

**yawn** (v.) bailler
**year** année
**yellow** jaune
**yesterday** hier
**yet** pourtant
**young** jeune
**yours** le, la, les tien(e)(s)/vôtre(s)
**yourself** toi-même
**yourselves** vous-mêmes
**youth** jeunesse
**yuck!** beurk!

## Z

**zoom** (v.) faire un gros plan

# Around the year

**THE FOUR SEASONS** spring - summer - autumn - winter

**THE TWELVE MONTHS** January - February - March - April - May - June - July
August - September - October - November - December

**THE SEVEN DAYS OF THE WEEK** Monday - Tuesday - Wednesday - Thursday
Friday - Saturday - Sunday

# Cardinal numbers

| | | |
|---|---|---|
| 1 one | 11 eleven | 21 twenty-one |
| 2 two | 12 twelve | 22 twenty-two |
| 3 three | 13 thirteen | 23 twenty-three |
| 4 four | 14 fourteen | 24 twenty-four |
| 5 five | 15 fifteen | 25 twenty-five |
| 6 six | 16 sixteen | 26 twenty-six |
| 7 seven | 17 seventeen | 27 twenty-seven |
| 8 eight | 18 eighteen | 28 twenty-eight |
| 9 nine | 19 nineteen | 29 twenty-nine |
| 10 ten | 20 twenty | 30 thirty, etc. |

10 ten 20 twenty 30 thirty 40 forty 50 fifty 60 sixty 70 seventy 80 eighty 90 ninety
100 one / a hundred 200 two hundred, etc.
152 one / a hundred and fifty-two, etc.
1,000 one / a thousand, 2,000 two thousand, etc.

# Ordinal numbers

| | | | |
|---|---|---|---|
| the first 1st | the eleventh 11th | the twenty-first 21st | the thirty-first 31st, etc. |
| the second 2nd | the twelfth 12th | the twenty-second 22nd | |
| the third 3rd | the thirteenth 13th | the twenty-third 23rd | |
| the fourth 4th | etc. | etc. | |
| the fifth 5th | | | |
| the sixth 6th | | | |
| the seventh 7th | | | |
| the eighth 8th | | | |
| the ninth 9th | | | |
| the tenth 10th | | | |

10th the tenth 20th the twentieth 30th the thirtieth 40th the fortieth 50th the fiftieth
100th the hundredth, etc.
152nd the hundred and fifty-second, etc.

## Références des textes

**p. 93** 10 Things to Help you Survive an Earthquake © American Red Cross ; **p. 131** The Cat and the Fox © Tony Ross, 1986, *Foxy Tables*, Ladybird Books Ltd UK. From a fable by La Fontaine ; **p. 133** The Guard Dog © Dick King- Smith, 1991, by Fox Busters Ltd ; **p. 137** Cats by Eleanor Farjeon *A Children's Zoo* © The Oxford University Press and David Higham Associates Ltd; Snail by John Drinkwater *A Children's Zoo* © Samuel French Limited ; **p. 138** The Pancake by Christina Rossetti, *Funny Rhymes* © Barbara Ireson,1980.

## Références des illustrations

**p. 3** © Bob Anderson / Masterfile ; **p. 5** Jason © Denis Boissavy / Pix; Clara © John Cannemoll / Australian Picture Library ; Pamela © Bertrand Gardel / HEMISPHERES ; Sean © Jess / Sipa Image ; Sean Connery © Steve Lemere / Sipa Press ; **pp.13, 16, 19** © Richard Greenhill ; **p. 23** 1,2 © Sally Greenhill ; 3 © Keith Gibson ; 4,6 © Richard Greenhill ; 5 © Sparham / Network / Rapho ; **p. 25** 1 © P. Carmichael / Cosmos ; 2 © Dorigny / Ilo / REA ; 3 © Collections / Brian Shuel ; 4 © D.R. Morris / Impact Visuals / Cosmos ; **p. 26** 1 © P. Bryans / Collections ; 2 © Lesley Howling / Collections ; 3 © Philippe Lissac / CIRIC ; **p. 27** Iqbal Masih © BLLF / Sygma ; paysage © Ed Kashi / Rapho ; **p. 28** 1, 2 © Keith Gibson ; 3 Richard Davis / Collections ; **p. 35** English school, The Bridgeman Art Library, London ; **pp. 36, 37** swimming, cycling, racing © Sally Greenhill ; jumping © R. Rowan / Ana; rugby © Vandystadt / A. Gadroffe ; football © All Sport photographic Ltd / Vandy stadt ; baseball © Steven E Sutton / Duomo / Vandystadt ; basketball ; tennis © Richard Greenhall ; **p. 38** 1 © Zefa Knoche / Hoa -Qui ; 2 C. Simon / SUNSET ; 3© Peter Cade / Photogram-Stone ; **p. 42** 1 © Giraudon ; 2 © Giraudon ; 3 © AKG Paris ; 4 Topham Picturepoint ; 5 © AKG Paris ; 6 © Camera Press London ; 7 © Keystone ; **p. 43** © Shakespeare English School 19th, The Bridgeman Art Library, London ; **p. 47** Koene / Explorer ; **p. 49** Mur d'Hadrien © M.Koene / Explorer ; Roman soldier © William Bell (1811-1890) National Trust Wallington Hall / The Bridgeman Art Library, London ; **p. 50** 1 © Ali Meyer / Artephot, 3 © AKG Paris ; 2, 4, 5 © Josse ; 6 © R.Burri / Magnum photos ; 7 © Stills ; 8 © Cherruault / Sipa Press ; **p. 55** © D. Reperant / Hoa-Qui ; **p. 57** © A.C. Poujoulat / Sdf / CIRIC ; **p. 62** Sally © Nik Wheeler / Corbis Sygma ; Charles © Ph. Frilet / Sipa Press ; Bill © Photofusion / Editing diffusion ; Charlotte © Helene Bamberger / Cosmos ; **pp. 62, 63, 70** Badges © The Guide Association / The Scout Association, London ; **p. 66** Code de la route © Crown copyright, reproduced with the Permission of the Controller of HMSO 1999 ; **p. 69** 1, 2 © Bureau mondial du scoutisme ; 3 © Imapress ; **pp. 70, 71** 1910, 2001 © The Guide Association / London ; **p. 72** 1 © Leverett Bradley / Stone ; 2 © V. Clément / Jerrican ; 3 © Perousse / NF / Hoa-Qui ; **p. 79** © K. Hessman / Archipress / Artur ; **p. 82** © Lorentz Gullachsen / Fotogram-Store ; **p. 84** 1 ® Hallmark Cards UK / Country Companions / TM Reproduced by kind permission ; 2,4 © Hanson White group Ltd. / 1994 ; 3 © Peter Cross / Gordon Fraser ; 5 © Quitting Hollywood; 6 © Simon Nevin / Camden Graphics Ltd ; 7 © The Andrew Brownsword Collection ; **p. 86** Disneyland © E. Valentin / Hoa-Qui ; Universal Studio © Henry Dietz / Corbis Sygma ; Redwood National Park © C. Hehlers / International ST / Cosmos ; **p. 91** © C Simonpietri / Corbis-Sygma ; **p. 92** San Fransisco © G. Sioen / Hoa-Qui ; Désert © John Mead / Science photo Library ; **p. 93** © A. Reiniger / Contact Press Images / 1994 ; **p. 94** 1 © Thomas / Jerrican ; 2 © Gus / Jerrican ; 3 © Bureau mondial du scoutisme ; 4 © Allard / REA ; 5 © Ph. Schuller / EDITING 9 ; **p. 101** © Japack / Sunset ; **p. 102** Les 3 frères Kennedy © Popperfoto / Cosmos ; Kirk Douglas © Regan / LFI / Cosmos ; Michael Douglas © MPA-Stills / All Action ; Michael et Janet Jackson © J. Gough /Celebrity Photos / Stills, **p. 103** Charlie Chaplin © Roger Viollet ; Geraldine Chaplin © Stéphane Benito / Imapress ; Jane Birkin et Charlotte Gainsbourg © Arnal / Charriau / Stills ; George Bush © Bob Daemmrich / Corbis Sygma ; **p. 106** 1 © Bruce Cotler / Globe Photos, INC / 1991 ; 2 © Richard Hamilton Smith / Corbis ; 3 © André SAS / Rapho ; 4 © J. Raga / Explorer ; **p. 107** Leeson / Sunset ; **p. 111** Jim Pickerell / Top ; **p. 114** Bill © D. Allain / Sunset; Mandy © Pictor International ; Melanie © Y. Forck / Global Picture / Hoa-Qui ; **p. 115** © Tannen Maury / IMAPRESS Cats by Eleanor Farjeon ; **p. 120** © Hachette Livre ; **p. 121** © Françoise Lemarchand ; **p. 123** © Mike Mc queen / Stone ; **p.161** G Bush junior, photo reprise de la p.103 ; **p.165** Jules César © Cat's Collection.

Achevé d'imprimer par Maury-Imprimeur S.A. - 45330 Malesherbes
Dépôt légal : 13090 - 07/2001. - Collection 85
Édition : 02 -12/5274/1